The Paradigm Prophecies

REFLECTIONS FOR HEALING

Jen,

Thank you for your healing help.

R. F. M.

RICHARD FRANCIS MOORE

Order this book online at www.trafford.com
or email orders@trafford.com

Most Trafford titles are also available at major online book retailers.

Print information available on the last page.

ISBN: 978-1-4907-7528-9 (sc)
ISBN: 978-1-4907-7496-1 (hc)
ISBN: 978-1-4907-7495-4 (e)

Library of Congress Control Number: 2016912020

Trafford rev.   01/12/2017

 www.trafford.com
North America & international
toll-free: 1 888 232 4444 (USA & Canada)
fax: 812 355 4082

Acknowledgments

I remain ever appreciative of the inspiration and extraordinary love of my beloved life partner, Ann, along with the indescribable gifts of my daughters, Catherine, Jennifer, and Mary. With similar gratitude, I recognize my loving parents, the late Frederick J. Moore and Norma Mycue-Moore, along with the strength of spirit demonstrated from the courageous lives of my grandmothers, Clara Frederick-Moore and Margaret Powers-Mycue. I would be remiss to not mention the positive sibling influences of five brothers (Paul, John, Fred, Joe, and Bob) and three sisters (Teresa, Chris, and Maria). Their collective influence on my personal growth during those formative years leaves a lifelong imprint that is valued. A special note of thanks to my sister Teresa for her various forms of proactive assistance and encouragement in regard to my writing, poetry, and speaking presentations.

I wholeheartedly thank the following individuals who have lovingly read various drafts of this unfolding book over a period of several years. Their edits and earnest feedback have kept me grounded and focused without ever discouraging my efforts. Their intuitive thoughts always encouraged me to clarify and express what was on my heart and mind. They include Barbara Basher, Carolyn Bray, Teresa Buchanan, Artie Lynnworth, Patricia Merino, Nancy Michalko, Ann Moore, Patrizia Porcari, Patsy Scala, Jimi Tutko, Paul and Jeannie Westmoore, and Maya Yonika.

I also remain grateful to the following institutions and the numerous friends and former colleagues for their expressions of informal yet important encouragement of my desire to examine various aspects of human healing.

1. SUNY at Buffalo (School Of Nursing)
2. Roswell Park Cancer Institute, Buffalo, New York
3. YMCA

The following individuals continue to have my sincere appreciation for their subtle and significant forms of support over time: Eric Alcott, Jane Armbruster, Paul Baker, Dawn Baumgartner, the late Robert Bieniek, and Sylvia Bieniek, Carolyn Bray, Kristen Brill, Christelle Brock, Dr. Jean Brown, Melanie Buhrmaster-Bunch, the late Pam Cardoza, Cathy Carfagna, Suzanne Chamberlain, Pamela Clark, Mary Cochrane, Ellen Cooper, the late Kathryn Costello, Ann Davis, Grace Dean, Fran and Kathy DeKalb, Marc Daul, Bill Dineen, Dave Draper, Cindy Eller, Mike Fellows, Carol

Fenstermacher, Deborah Finnell, the late Patricia H. Garman, Mary Glenn, Maureen Hammett, Barbara Hole, Gayle Hutton, Donna Juenker, Dr. Coletta Klug, Tom LaFluer, Amy Jo Lauber, Mark Mahoney, Kathryn Majewicz, Mike Marrone, Fred Moore, Maria Murphy, Cookie Mycue-McGaha, Mary Ellen Nelson, Sally Rice, Pam Robinson, Mary Ann Rogers, Diana Edwards-Rowland, Leslie Russo, Sally Sams, Lynn Santa Lucia, William Schmidtke, Loralee Sessana, Mary Ann Sharrow, Rachel Stack, Donna Tyrpak, Deb Scott, Carol Vanini, Fran Vaughan, Kim Venti, Kathleen Wiater, Minnie Saleh-Wyse, and Leigh Yates.

The views expressed in this work are solely those of the author and do not necessarily reflect the views of those whom are acknowledged for their general encouragement to write.

With the passage of time, please accept my apology to other individuals whom I no doubt failed to note.

Dedication

This book is dedicated to any individual who has ever made the courageous choice of pursuing a deeper healing for the wounds incurred in their lives and is equally dedicated to all those who will make such a conscious choice in the future. The intentions of this book also support the healing energies of family, friends, communities, and all the countries encircling our globe, thus nurturing the entire population of the planet now and forevermore.

This includes a special dedication in memory of Dr. Mecca S. Cranley, the late dean of the School of Nursing (1991-2006) for the SUNY at Buffalo. Dr. Cranley was a powerful leader and a voice of wisdom and healing in the field of nursing and beyond. As nurse and mother, she and her husband, Ed (an engineer), proudly nurtured their seven children while providing exemplary leadership in their professional lives. As both my boss and friend for some twelve years, I learned much about healing from her that benefited my entire family. The personal and professional courage she demonstrated before succumbing to cancer was inspiring and insightful in regard to providing healing lessons for us all. I believe she would be proud of the healing intentions expressed in this book.

Ultimately, this writing is dedicated to all healers, both conventional and alternative, from traditional treatments to modern modalities, from ancient therapies to clinical trials, or the scientific to the spiritual. Be it public or private, professional or personal, we all have an undeniably powerful role in taking responsibility for healing ourselves, each other, and our planet. Blessings to all along this journey in life that we ultimately share together!

My special intention is to dedicate this book to individuals born or raised in the new millennium. These generations will help to further reawaken humanity to advance our healing beyond our limited understandings to date. All humanity will benefit from their visions of new prophetic paradigms, based upon revelations from newly unearthed truths.

Contents

Prologue

Understanding Diversity

Writing with an intention to support individuals in their own healing process (as everyone will need multiple healings throughout our lives), I cite three premises of this:

1. By the very act of sharing the collective wisdom of personal stories with each other, our healing process can be positively influenced when we earnestly seek to *understand* and examine how we all interrelate as part of the human family.

2. Self-healing implies a free-will decision by the individual to open oneself to a process that privately invites one to examine differing perspectives on life. Such a process creates a safe place for individual readers to question their own indoctrinations, traditions, and understandings they currently live by. In this place, we can assess answering for ourselves the effectiveness of the beliefs and times in which we now live.

3. This approach intentionally presents opposing outlooks and paradoxical points of view. This offers us the opportunity to step outside our "predictable" reactions that are often automatically generated from the deeply rooted conditionings of our own heritage. Our background is important, but it often requires us to publicly endorse old values we may or may not totally agree with over time. Exploring the experiences of others may provide insights that could potentially benefit us as we declare our own freedom and independent life journey.

The Birth of This Book and How It Came to Fruition

What began with assembling a book of inspired poetry gradually evolved into combining prose to more fully express and support any individual who seeks healing in their life. These individual paths paradoxically reveal how much we also share in common with one another. By utilizing a fusion of prose and poetry in a unique format, it can read like a novel and also serve as a book of meditations providing poetic reflections at the end of each chapter. Picturing the prose symbolically as the structural physical body of the text, it is framed by the poetry's more mystical imagery of spirit speaking intuitively from a power deep within us. (These poems came to me from within a powerfully creative wellspring of inspiration, which I was often moved to write after listening to individuals share their intense personal stories of healing). Each chapter concludes with a short optional worksheet to privately journal any beneficial observations of the healing journey of your own life.

The Sources of This Privileged Material

During my thirty-five-year career of securing volunteers and raising funds to support healthy causes, I was privileged to hear many individuals share their personal experiences of healing. In this professional capacity, I served in positions of leadership for several significant wellness and health care institutions that included the School of Nursing for SUNY at Buffalo, Roswell Park Cancer Institute, and the YMCA. My work entailed surveying many community and corporate leaders with related strategic planning interviews, in addition to thousands of healing practitioners (primarily nurses), patients, and their families in forty-two states. By sharing some of their selected stories, I am better able to convey diverse perspectives and many different dimensions of our human healing experience, including my own.

These individual surveys influenced my personal growth as I gradually opened myself up to utilizing healers outside the conventional circle of health care providers I was accustomed to. My search for healing solutions slowly expanded beyond the mainstream protocols of Western medicine to include practitioners in many holistic and alternative therapies. These practitioners and clients candidly shared how they personally benefited from various healing arts as they worked through their own injuries and illnesses. By sharing with you these select personal stories (often anonymously for privacy purposes) to better understand recovery and wellness, I trust it may be beneficial to your own journey of restoration, renewal, and healing. It was for this express purpose of healing for which I was given permission in the first place to share their observations.

As I wrote about these privileged insights, I also drew upon some relevant experiences from my own personal health challenges over time, gradually integrating some of their counsel and wisdom into my own life process. I soon discovered that not only was my family benefiting from these incredibly diverse insights and unfamiliar therapies but also they were now contributing to my own personal growth and healing. As their collective counsel began to cover a wider range of our human experiences, the implied advice often challenged my usual comfort zone far beyond my earlier understandings and preconceptions. Conventional and alternative remedies initially included areas of physical concern, later followed by inquiries of the emotional, psychological, and spiritual dimensions of life. Eventually, I chose to explore more deeply the metaphysical and spiritual aspects of life relating to healing the human spirit.

While interviewing strangers regarding healing topics was one thing professionally, reflecting upon the healing aspects of my personal nature was more challenging. Examples of my most traumatic and profoundly personal experiences in relation to healing include the following:

- the sudden death of my father in my adolescence
- the accidental shooting and death of my thirteen-year-old brother
- my mom's death from cancer
- another brother's fatal heart attack at a young age
- my wife and children's successful outcomes from a decade of tumors and cancers
- a heart attack, joint surgery, and chronic congenital back conditions, to cite just a few
- my wife's strokes during the writing of this book

In sharing a wide array of outside perspectives alongside my own deeply personal experiences, I endeavor to bring to life for the reader this book's fundamental focus to support an individual's healing as part of their lifelong growth process.

Naturally, we all are likely to have traumatic occurrences in our life, our families, and our communities. This is one key point of my writing—to notice and observe how much we share in common despite our unique backgrounds. Beyond the usual personal challenges of our physical existence, it only takes a moment of reflection to see how so many others around the world suffer enormously tragic and often unnecessary hardships each day, be it from war or so many other natural disasters.

Being cognizant of these global sufferings, I often remain grateful in retrospect for my comparatively less severe adversity. Regardless of the severity of one's suffering and injury, no pain can be discounted or compared to that of others on some Richter scale of suffering. Everyone's pain, loss, and injury are a unique and undeniable part of their own life journey. These circumstances have undoubtedly shaped all of us, one way or another, and can potentially offer positive guidance upon our ongoing path, guiding conscious new choices toward personal peace and healing.

The Structure of the Book

The book contains ten chapters, each offering observations and perspectives around a few familiar aspects of our human experience. Each one intermittently visits various stages of our natural growth and maturation processes in an attempt to increase understanding of ourselves and our world. The real-life experiences are followed by related poetry that serves as an informal meditation on these different dimensions of our shared humanity. The chapters are divided into three distinct acts. (Although not a play, they do in a sense represent our very real human drama.) They deal with:

1. <u>The past</u>
   This includes an exploration of the nature of a healthy declaration of our *independence*.
2. <u>The present</u>
   Here I examine humanities growing into a healthier form of *interdependence*.
3. <u>The future</u>
   The third section addresses the aspect of declaring our innate *divinity*.

By purposefully approaching this book, you can embark on your own private journey, freeing yourself to reflect outside the usual forces that daily influence you. Here you may freely choose and safely look back upon your life to honestly acknowledge *past* experiences and recognize one's *present* circumstances. From this vantage point, you might begin focusing on a key purpose of this book, which is ultimately for each individual to envision and then create the healthy *future* they have long desired or only have dreamed of. While working on one's own health needs to come first, invariably, it possess the potential to help others in your immediate sphere and beyond.

Clarification of the Book's Intentions

As stated, these writings support human healing at many levels. While considering many contrasting viewpoints, they are not intended to advance any specific belief system or any political, religious, or philosophical preference. Bearing this in mind, I encourage the reader to set aside any defensive resistance to differing points of view, knowing that our journey simply seeks to *understand* another's circumstances. (One need not necessarily agree with it, and no one is being asked to change their mind or feelings.) The journey on this road permits one to privately reflect upon them and possibly learn something from their experience. Thus, the subject matter has no religious, cultural, political, economic, or social agenda to promote. These stories are presented only to help us listen to others first, which can free us to better hear our inner voice and intuitive wisdom.

A secondary intention is to provide a reader with an informal *process* for self-reflection that may benefit your personal healing. I have repeatedly observed that when we earnestly pause to simply grasp and *understand* another's circumstances and beliefs, we unleash a positive power within our being. Standing in another's shoes can equip us with insights that foster our own growth and maturation. For instance, who among us maintains all the same convictions about life at age 10, 20, 30, 50, 60, and beyond? If one actually never changed a single belief during their lifetime, it might someday serve as a source of individual regret rather than celebrated as having been loyal to a fault.

To best assist you on this journey, I encourage all to examine their inherited values and indoctrinations from the special heritage and traditions of your own birth. Without judgment of good, bad, right, or wrong, simply observe your own culture, country, religion, etc. From this acknowledgment, you can begin to observe all those who differ from your own special uniqueness as a person. This reflection will serve as a guide for you to enter a pathway for a personal healing journey.

Restating that I propose no monolithically righteous viewpoint, I do repeat the assertion that by seeking to understand the realities of others, we can reduce much negative energy in our life and in those around us. Such negativities include misunderstandings that often lead us to fear, paranoia, self-righteousness, anger, hatred, jealousy, and aggression, to cite a few. (These elements often injure us and others and do *not* promote healing.)

While there may be a time and a place for everything, the unchecked societal expressions of these tendencies inevitably manifest themselves in the collective act of war. Make no mistake about it: war is always the end result of millions of individually accumulated negative acts and energies. These tendencies are best dealt with beforehand, just as you would prefer to deal early on with any disease that afflicted you or a loved one. While the book is not focused on the topic of war, it is intentionally used to demonstrate an extreme example of the importance of taking individual responsibility for our healing. In this context, we will examine how self-healing can actually be a practical and pragmatic act of good citizenship that spreads healing to others.

I would further caution the reader to resist any initial temptation to dismiss this text as an impractical or theoretical document (e.g., "can't we all just get along"). If one can stay focused on the intentional simplicity of the aforementioned purposes, you may just discover profound revelations miraculously arising from within you as you continue to move through your own life journey. The question will always be, will you move through with awareness and freedom, or will you simply watch the sunset with the convictions of your inherited birth circumstances? It is with faith and optimism that I share these stories to benefit your own thoughts on healing yourselves, your families, and inevitably, our world.

In summary, this writing is an open invitation for anyone to embark upon a journey of discovery into their own freedom of thought and their personal healing power within. Along the journey, I share many diverse personal stories I was so privileged to hear. Over time, these shared lessons unexpectedly began to form some common themes. These life experiences came from individuals in many socioeconomic groupings, ethnicities, religions, and cultures. Despite covering the spectrum of conservative and liberal political persuasions, they often echoed some similar chords.

One common theme centered on the search for new perspectives and viewpoints to advance humanity beyond many current global dilemmas and paralysis. Thus, this writing encourages everyone in formulating new thoughts and insights on healing for your individual lives while also considering their relationship to our connected path as a human race. Interestingly, one of the book's unintended suggestions is to ease the rat race, if you will, intentionally pausing to slow down and quiet ourselves. By learning to pause in silence, we might open ourselves to observe how our unique individual journeys may be impacting the whole of humanity.

In the end, the book poses fundamental questions for each individual reader to answer for themselves, such as:

- Going forward, what facets of life might you choose to consider changing to better serve your personal health and well-being?
- Can you identify specific aspects of this life that you feel could be changed or improved upon to help yourself individually or perhaps benefit all of humankind?

As we mature over the decades from child to teen, adult, and elderly, which one of us has not made course corrections in our own life to any desired destination, be it geographical, professional, or personal? As humanity crosses the threshold of a new millennium, we are accompanied with the increasing ability to easily communicate globally (e.g., Internet, travel, etc.). Consequently, we all share an awesome opportunity (to communicate positively or negatively) to chart our common course as one human race that was not available to us just decades earlier. Our ability to heal injury is critical to all!

What new paradigms of understanding might help us? Let us explore.

***"Grant that I may not so much seek to be understood as to* understand."**

—*Francis of Assisi*

ACT I: THE PAST

A Declaration of Independence

(Chapters 1 to 5)

Since we all seemingly understand that the past is over, unalterable and arguably unchangeable, it beckons us to explore one obvious contradiction in human behavior. Why is it that we appear to spend so much time revisiting days gone by to dwell upon the reruns of our lives? For what reasons do we choose to effectively replay bygone moments? Since we have all done this, there is no judgment implied, but it is only an attempt to understand our own reasons for choosing to spend our time in this manner. Act I helps us examine these questions from the following three (3) foundational perspectives:

I. Our inherited **collective history as a human race** (What we term as current events could also be considered as our unconscious allegiance to old patterns condemning us to chronic repetition of past.)

II. Our **individual experiences that we all share in common** (This pertains to the journey from birth to death.)

III. Our **uniquely individual journey as one of billions of individual beings** (This will be demonstrated by sharing personal stories from various sources.)

By first identifying some common ground we all share, we can heighten our awareness as we proceed revisiting some of the past together. Beginning with some familiar frames of reference from public life, we also integrate aspects of our individual experiences that are familiar to us. Acknowledging some common understandings of our human histories, we can compare various accounts regarding our origins of creation from the darkness and out of nothingness (e.g., from Genesis, to big bang, and beyond). In examining human nature through these well-known religious and cultural traditions and more recent scientific discovery, we can begin to review our many past footprints in the history of the human wilderness. I believe these vantage points all help bear witness to our intuitive and marvelous ability to move out from the darkness toward the light of a brighter future.

While this is a practical approach in one sense, it also provides us a parallel opportunity to at least reflect upon a more mystical source of an inner light so often referenced in almost every tradition. Depending upon your own reflective journey, discovering such an inner strength might provide a valuable resource in dealing with the well-documented difficulties of our constantly changing existence. By shedding new light upon the aging foundations of our past, we may potentially free ourselves to rise to greater heights as we rise up and choose to move forward in constructing new foundational truths in building for future generations.

Whether we do this with courage and grace in the current age is an opportunity we have been entrusted with, and like it or not, it is a responsibility we all share together. As is always true, one is free to passively ignore the choices of changing times, but at what peril?

Proceeding onward, one might notice that our story of who we each appear to be identified by others or by our own ego's self-perception does not fully describe who we truly are as individuals in the deepest private sense. While our unique identities serve a relevant purpose in our daily lives, these assumptions and descriptions can lessen in their importance as we age. As we become increasingly aware of our nature, we stand to discover (actually rediscover) that our *true story* is an important part of a more timeless universal experience. Deep down, we all have implanted within us a sense of being both a unique creation while also sharing in common an even greater global destiny. If we can come to understand this one example of our dual reality (duality), we might empower ourselves to consciously and confidently move ahead in a more positive way. Increasingly, we can experience the joy implicit in sharing our true destiny! Shared experiences are a powerful force. Just consider for instance a dynamic and emotionally moving concert or an exciting sports event where tens of thousands of people join to ecstatically celebrate living. Some specific examples of these three foundational perspectives follow.

I. A Sampling of Our Collective History as a Human Race

A recognizable snapshot of a shared public experience includes the unanimous declaration of the thirteen colonies as the sovereign United States of America.

"When, in the course of human events, it becomes necessary for one people to dissolve the political bonds which have connected them with another, and to assume among the powers of the earth, the separate and equal station to which the laws of nature and of nature's God entitle them, a decent respect to the opinions of mankind requires that they should declare the causes which impel them to the separation."

"We hold these truths to be self-evident, that all men are created equal, that they are endowed by their Creator with certain unalienable rights that among these are life, liberty and the pursuit of happiness. That to secure these rights, governments are instituted among men, deriving their just powers from the consent of the governed. That whenever any form of government becomes destructive to these ends, it is the right of the people to alter or to abolish it, and to institute new government, laying its foundation on such principles and organizing its powers in such form, as to them shall seem most likely to affect their safety and happiness. Prudence, indeed, will dictate that governments long established should not be changed for light and transient causes; and accordingly, all experience hath shown that mankind are more disposed to suffer, while evils are sufferable, than to right themselves by abolishing the forms to which they are accustomed."

Harboring Hope

This cherished American document, a prophetic paradigm,
Speaks to mankind in declaring this foundation of liberty.
Yet it unites us by separating both church and state,
Joining us together, removing ties that bind religious debates.

A universally cherished statement echoes worldwide for all equally created beings to hear.
This single declaration inspires all humankind with hope, by virtue of our common origins.
Our divine birthright of freedom thus birthed a nation yet without regard to a nationality.
Drawing its strength from the diverse sources documented by our historical volatility.
Contradictions abounded alongside this vision with a balance of power in mind,
Combining to create an ingenious foundation for the future of humankind.

United in this diversity, this statement against separation beckons our liberating reunion,
Appealing to all souls around the globe in one anticipated union.
This is the genius and vision of these prophetic American documents,
Perhaps more philosophical than political, more spiritual than social,
It is little wonder that leagues of nations continue to unite nations,
To give birth to immigrants visions of our original source of oneness.

II. Elements of Our Individual Experiences That We Share in Common

Our birth and death serve as visibly obvious bookends of our transitory physical existence, but what of the deeper nature of what lies in-between the experiences of our personal and multidimensional lives? Noticing the most basic aspects of our individual lives cannot help but lead us to observe and galvanize a shared sense of kinship to the human family. The essential requirement for food and water easily demonstrate the most common nourishment we all need from Mother Earth for our mutual sustenance. Such snapshots are simple, but they help us see our need to share resources and picture new images of our evolving unity with each new earthly revolution.

photo by Richard Moore

Observe how maps are forever redrawn. Witness how humankind now finds itself bordering on unlimited potential. Boundaries are expanding beyond previously perceived limitations of the past times or a future in space. Overcoming perceptions of an old world, we may now see through illusions where populations appeared forever separated by oceans of adversity. By acknowledging universally outdated notions of a flat world that never really did hold water, we can better envision what lies beyond the present view of navigating our personal stormy seas with greater possibilities. Can our commonly shared experiences contribute to a shared vision for our future world? In contrast, can celebrating our individual uniqueness also help us see the link to our common bonds, so creatively exemplified as strung together by our DNA?

We need to comprehend that our DNA lives beyond our merely biological understandings to also symbolically view these genealogical building blocks anew and better redefined as:

Do **N**ot **A**gain choose to be separated as a human family . . .

. . . and further wrapping ourselves around this double helix as our **D**estiny of **N**ever-ending **A**ffinity!

III. Everyone's Unique Personal Journey

Integrated into this book's first act is the prose and poetry relating to my personal story. Within our singular individual rhythms, we sometimes experience discordant periods while at other times, we feel sweetly synchronized with all of life. I have certainly felt the elation and deflation of this dichotomy.

On the positive end, I have been blessed with so many glorious aspects of joy in this life. One reason is that early on, I was privileged to have been exposed to many diverse influences. Specifically, I genuinely benefited from exposure to the world's many faith traditions, each with its own cherished written words. Personally knowing individuals whose loving examples spoke positively to living their respective faith traditions with integrity also assisted me in developing a genuine love for all humankind. Over time, I was further privileged to listen in person to the Dalai Lama, Billy Graham, and Pope John Paul II, where I observed both the blessings and unholy blindness of institutionalized religions.

While I have certainly benefited from positive expressions of various faith communities, I have also witnessed disturbing negativities. Here I have often heard sermons of separation preached over unity, human hatred sown by promoting fear of differences rather than demonstrating faith in a professed loving creator, let alone loving one's fellow man. Such contradictions eventually drew me to read many modern-day messengers whose writings to me reflect a divine inspiration to humankind, not unlike the revered ancient scribes of the world's religions.

Authors Deepak Chopra, Neale Donald Walsch, Caroline Myss, Marianne Williamson, Eckhart Tolle, Ken Carey, Louise Hay, Esther and Jerry Hicks, Gary Renard, Leo Hartong, David Hawkins, Daphne Rose Kingma, Diana Richardson, David Deida, Lynn Taggart, and Mantak Chia are just some of these present-day prophets whose insights have touched me and millions more. These authors significantly contributed to my growth and development in the same manner as many of the primary influences of my youth had. These included the courageous twentieth-century examples of Mahatma Gandhi and Dr. Martin Luther King Jr. All of these authors have validated and reaffirmed for me the path which has always been unfolding in the experiences of my own life. I smile widely as I look back and see how hindsight can provide us with a meaningful panoramic view, regardless of whether our experiences were good, bad, or indifferent.

In the midst of my retrospective smiling, I seriously see that we are living at a time of an emerging awareness and a shift in consciousness unfolding around the globe. It is simply a great time to be alive, perilous as it may also be! Significant signs are everywhere. Witness the proliferation of authors offering insights and understandings of such rapid historical changes and their crystallization of our ability to freely choose calamity or creativity. Evolving insights on our spiritual nature alongside miraculous scientific and technological advancement serve each of us with a great opportunity to revisit our personal past and cocreate our inevitable future together.

With increased awareness, we can better use our rather recently acquired freedoms to also consciously choose our individual path. At the same time, we are collectively deciding our planet's future and the future of generations to come. Perhaps at this moment, our generation can bring a renewed meaning to the term "the greatest generation." For example, consider the undeniable intent of those who sacrificed their lives to provide a better future for us. Such were the heroic sacrifices of our forefathers whose generation once expressed quite categorically their desired goal in fighting World War I as "a war to end all wars."

What I am asking here is simply this:

Does anyone truly believe in their heart that our fathers, mothers, grandparents, or any of our ancestors would now want their offspring to be fighting a WWIII? If they could come back and speak to us from the grave today, what do *you* think would they say to us about repeating the past? Perhaps the lessons from our personal and public past can now contribute to creating new approaches for our collective inspiration. If, for instance, Northern Ireland (after centuries of hurtful and hateful repetition) can courageously turn down a new road of hope and peace for previously divided populations, can we not piece together new paths of understanding to other puzzling problems on our planet? Even the globe's borders appear as shapes used in a jigsaw puzzle! Can we *think, pray, and act* now to begin solving this together?

In summarizing the *past* in the first section of this book, I pause to share one of my relevant holistic healing pursuits. I recall attending a unique healing experience led by a shamanic healer who turned out to be profoundly spiritual as well. This particular experience was a very simple spiritual ritual consisting of a meditation where I wrote down in advance my most painful or disturbing memories. It culminated in a prayerful time to acknowledge their hurt, followed by a releasing of painful remaining emotions by literally lighting a fire to my list, and in effect release past pains. The noticeable result was a freeing up of my energies to move forward with my life in a most positive way. When I now recall my past, it no longer has any negative or haunting power over me, but I actually draw energy and strength from my understanding of how even perceived mistakes and unwanted negative experiences have served me well in terms of my formative personal and spiritual growth. With this understanding, forgiveness began to flow as a natural outcome, and so did my personal healing.

I share this healing session to demonstrate how our uniquely personal past can reveal new insights in the present. Our past need not paralyze us but can be used to benefit us in a healthy manner. Our life lessons have the potential to reveal fresh observations of what we share in common as a human race. This simple understanding is critical to our healing, and it blesses us with the ability to respect differing individual paths in our present times.

Appreciation of this dynamic offers us wisdom to quietly witness how various nations, cultures, religions, and other institutions can all contribute to divine insights beneficial for the future of all. Herein lies the link where initial individual healing precedes the collective healing of all peoples and our planet. Many parts all serve one body.

Poetry can sometimes serve to transport us far above the world's daily obstacles and routines. For example, when we take a moment to rise above any chaos and calmly look down to view life, such a lofty perspective can provide opportunities to observe openings in the clouds. As we peer through these veiled illusions of an often foggy physical world, a panoramic view can reveal clearer insights into our true eternal nature. In doing so, we become the key to opening the door on a journey into a special dimension within everyone. As others observe us living a more peaceful and joyful life, they too will be positively impacted by our change.

Embarking upon this reflective journey, here's a quick reminder to permit yourself to read the prose in a manner that translates to the corresponding relevance of your own stories and your own life in this world. (As a reader, you might even consider keeping your own progressive journal as you read any relevant passages or reflect upon the poetry that might assist you in charting your own lifelong journey.)

Chapters 1–5 focus upon the *past* and our historical origins of dependency, sometimes enforced or even willingly accepted. These chapters present many cross-sections of daily life in helping us observe our past in a healthy manner that can empower us to face the present and future with greater clarity. So with a conscious declaration of our personal independence, we prepare ourselves to travel farther down a road of greater awareness and truer freedom. Along the way, remember that you are ever free to turn down any road on your explorations in life. May whatever roads you choose be a blessing, and above all, enjoy the journey!

Photo by Richard F Moore

Chapter 1

In the Darkness of Illusions

Understanding First Exposures

"Give your servant therefore an understanding mind" (1 Kings 3:9).

Past perspectives may or may not be affecting your outlook in life. Nevertheless, it is a worthy exercise to attempt identifying potential benefits or liabilities of maintaining allegiance to our previous teachings and understandings. Examining some common aspects of our universal human experience alongside the unique paths we are all share on our personal journey in life can be revealing. While our paths may be unique, at some point it seems most of us come to report periods of personal darkness that can also be related to the public experiences we share in as part of human history (e.g., a natural disaster, a world war, etc.). When periods of darkness do descend on our personal lives, they can serve as an invitation for us to reassess or reaffirm our beliefs, values, and overall understanding of life in some way, shape, or form.

Just as newborns first open their eyes and are greeted to a blurry view, so it is that our first exposure to any emotional darkness may require time for us to adjust to the dark before we are able to clearly see again and find new perspective.

During one's lifetime, we all eventually pass through what has often be termed a "dark night of the soul." Whether we express it in more common phrases such as "down on one's luck," "clinically depressed," or "just having the blues," their meaning is similar. The term "dark night" originated from the writings of the sixteenth-century Catholic poet St. John of the Cross. Over time, it has also been referenced by various spiritual traditions worldwide. Wikipedia defines it as "an expression used to describe a phase in a person's *spiritual* life, a *metaphor* for a certain loneliness and desolation." It further cites the Buddhist expression of "raising great doubt" as another understanding of this concept.

By any definition, we all experience dark times of separation not only physically but also, more powerfully, through a sense of isolation in mind and spirit. In this darkened state, we can lose perspective and fail to notice those who may be close by and present for us. Conversely, it may also be accurate that while we sense the multitudes of people surrounding us, we assume they all have little or no understanding of our despair, and in this context, we may remain alone in a sort of self-imposed isolation.

An essential observation of my own experiences is that in retrospect, this state of darkness is *not* our reality; it is only a powerful illusion of separation. I have chosen to accept the existence of this experience as an opportunity for personal growth, if we can only see through the illusory trick being played upon our senses. But how can we see though it?

Let us try and contrast this view to our dark first exposure, using a different lens by focusing at a more lighthearted and humorous exploration of this theme. In the film *Groundhog Day*, actor Bill Murray expresses utter exhaustion with his own form of darkness displayed in the futility of his character's endlessly repetitive existence. So it is that I mercifully begin exploring dark experiences with a smile as I later share my own equivalent of a dark night of the soul.

I have certainly experienced that the very act of honestly sharing our seemingly negative experiences with each other is one way we discover we are not alone! Here is where hindsight can lead us down a road where positive enlightenment can more likely unfold. Our candid realism with each other can prove more believable and credible in helping to see beyond some of our often personal Illusions and crumbling foundations of our institutions and present world. With clearer vision, we will be more capable of looking directly at our demons and laugh at the darkness. Just as we now understand and laugh at our childhood fear of the dark, as adults, we can overcome fearing similar illusions as are daily presented in the mass media. Unrelenting negative reports are portrayed with melodramatic manipulation, drawing conclusions as if the sky is falling.

In short, it is increasingly apparent that this chronic emphasis on crying wolf in popular culture can increase our personal anxiety levels, especially if that is what we are choosing to hear or even believe daily. This is particularly true in regard to the unrelenting assault that television and radio news has placed before us with a pervasive intrusion into our public spaces. It seems wherever you are these days (e.g., in a restaurant, in the doctors' office, in an airport), an uninvited and large HD TV monitor presents us exaggerated, immature, and distorted falsehoods. Broadcasting at an intrusive high-decibel level, these reports can deafen us to hearing our own quiet truth within. This point is captured well by the infamous big brother in George Orwell's book *1984* and even more effectively expressed by the late George Harrison in his musical composition "Devil's Radio." If you can, it is worth a listen.

It's white and black like industrial waste
Pollution of the highest degree
You wonder why I don't hang out much

I wonder how you can't see
He's in the films and songs and on all your magazines
It's everywhere that you may go
The devil's radio
Oh yeah, gossip . . .
                    (George Harrison, "Devil's Radio")

Despite the reality of cynical circumstances, our focus here remains abundantly hopeful in looking beyond negative appearances. By acknowledging and confronting our darkest personal and public forebodings, we will better position ourselves to unveil our future vision of healing. Seeing through any facades we may identify can provide a clearer picture of reality in the light of day, living in a land we can help create to more fully enjoy life in the present moment.

By 2008, my three children were raised, and I had just completed the professional commitment I once made to the University of Buffalo. With the support of my beloved wife, I decided to take the present moment as an opportunity to pause and review my life and maybe even write about it. But what would I write about? Accepting the risk inherent in any uncertainty, I decided to leave my profession, cash in some retirement savings early, and risk exploring my now uncertain future. In this reflective state of mind, I would drive coast to coast, covering some seven thousand miles on my odyssey across the USA and back home. Along the way, I was able to visit dozens of old friends, family, and former colleagues. I was heartened as they warmly took me in for a stay and permitted me to share my concerns, desires, and dreams. In the safety of their homes, I was able to secure their insightful support as we discussed my still vague pursuits.

My three-month journey would take me through heavy snows, sleet, freezing rain, heavy thunderstorms, dense fog, and 120-degree desert heat. My final road test would then take me through a powerful gauntlet of springtime storms across the heartland of the country. It is here I literally dodged several tornados to avoid ominous forecasts on my route home. I experienced a close call one day as one of those black prairie skies seemingly came out of nowhere, descending upon me in what seemed to be mere seconds. Gusting furiously, they buffeted my vehicle with great force as hail and waves of rain fell so fast that I had no choice but to pull off the road. At this point, no matter how much I slowed down or how fast my windshield wipers went, seeing clearly was still impossible. After my departure in March, I did arrive home safely with spring in full bloom and ready for my own new season of growth.

I utilize this imagery to help get us on the same page as we begin to visualize our progressive journey of human healing together. In this context, the chapter represents the emotional equivalent of "we all weather the personally threatening storms of life." To help place you into this environment, I now proceed with the first of several biographical vignettes that will occasionally precede selected poems in certain chapters. It is my hope that these biographical briefs (of me and others whom I interviewed) will more clearly connect the stories written in prose, alongside their inspired poetic meditations.

Like the first exposure of an old photographic, all illusions eventually shed their filmy quality and reveal a clearer picture of reality. Similarly, our journey within might expose before your eyes a revealing glimpse of your truer inner self, just as you have witnessed the sun break through the temporary shadows in the greater world we all share together.

Storm Warnings: (watercolor R.F.Moore)   *Spring storm (photo R.F.Moore)*

Biographical Background

Born in 1951, I was a typical post-war child (aka a baby boomer) about to experience the extreme conformity of the 1950s replete with the repressive prevailing political, social, and religious indoctrinations of that time. This set of values was particularly geared to white Americans and certainly more toward males than females. The 1960s would follow with a fury that was the antitheses of rigidity, marked by revolutionary new thinking that shook the foundation of many of our institutions to near ruins and, in some cases, were literally burned to the ground. It was a decade of dichotomy where we could fly to the moon and back in a giant leap for mankind and, at the same time, come to the brink of nuclear war! At least I was not alone during the escalating birth rate explosion though I often felt emotionally lonely within. From an early age, I never felt comfortable with any allegiance to extreme groups, liberal or conservative. On the other hand, I felt the deep and impending need for change in our world, whether I liked it or not! I think at an unconscious level, I knew the world was out of balance and that somehow this term "balance" would be an important part of my seeking, be it political, religious, social, or even interpersonal with my eventual romantic relationships with the feminine gender.

The third of nine children in a typically humble Irish Catholic household, I experienced an identity with much love, and I benefited from a sense of belonging with more food, clothing, shelter, and education than most children on the planet could dream of. This, of course, represented a significant improvement over the upbringing of my parents and previous immigrant generations, a fact I continue to appreciate. Rightfully acknowledging the sacrificial efforts of my parents' hard work, I also felt the reality of dysfunctional influences, ranging from frustrated parents whose church dictated to them a literal teaching that sexual relations were *only* "right" under God's law if done with the intent of procreation. Other pursuits of sexual pleasure were sinful. This was but one example of rigid religious underpinnings that would eventually come to affect family members and friends in untold repressed ways.

Add to this the backdrop of 1950s parenting norms that included regular belt beatings that were also reinforced in the parochial school as nuns and priests also utilized physical punishment, with the explanation that such discipline might keep us from eternal hell. Alongside this dogma existed cultural norms that were equally terrorizing with a fear of certain communist invasion; nuclear bomb drills were conducted in the school basement with warnings to keep your hands under the desk so as to prevent having your exposed fingers unnecessarily burned off. A paradigm that was the norm then is quite insanely absurd now, but it is so silently terrorizing to a child being asked to accept this casual drill as part of the school day!

While these biographical footnotes are purposeful, I must balance them by acknowledging the many blessings and benefits I also received from my parents, my family, and a church community that also possessed a wealth of loving attributes that positively served my life over time. In truth, all of our experiences include downsides that present us with an opportunity for our growth, development, and enlightenment if we choose to use them as such.

For the meaningful purposes of this first chapter, let's fast forward my young life to the years 1968–1972. In this brief time, the security of my life was radically removed, first in the public domain with the assassinations of Dr. Martin Luther King and Senator Bobby Kennedy, who arguably would likely have been elected the next president. One year later, I would be called out of school and told that my father (only fifty years old) died unexpectedly at home from an undetected cardiovascular problem. The ramifications of my mom as a widow with no advanced education or employment history were daunting, to say the least, for all of us. As my mom slowly recovered, she did her best to keep our family together. Two years later, my thirteen-year-old brother was accidentally shot and killed in a neighborhood home as a friend fatally played with a loaded hunting rifle.

These were unimaginably crushing losses for us all, and they came at the same time as former classmates arrived home in coffins from Vietnam. The killings of Kent State students seemed to serve as a brutal exclamation point to the end of my youth and the death of youthful idealism that had begun with President Kennedy's assassination in 1963. This period of national and personal darkness is where my journey proceeded with fear and an oppressive uncertainty!

Whether or not you have experienced some similar darkness or pain, let us continue our private inward journey. Reiterating the purpose of the following poetic meditations are intended for the reader's quiet reflection. They are expressed in a language of the heart that yearns to transcend topical words to heal the less visible deeper wounds we may carry.

Substituted

Truth is often slowly subverted,
Illusions are imported, spinning is exported.
A conscience once exhorted, is now exiled and extorted.

As populations are suppressed, our spirits become stressed.
With logic increasingly convoluted,
Systematically realigned, thinking is polluted,
Confusing the context of life, truth is cleverly substituted.

Despite being well educated,
To illusions we become dedicated.
Leaders ingratiated, and later self-congratulated,
As humanity hungers, increasingly emaciated.

Soul and body come to lie in waste and destitution,
As we legislate and litigate without real resolution,
Politically polite citizens have straight postures corrected,
Conforming to these institutions we crookedly erected.

Love is tough, a new slant redefined,
Old penal codes are now freshly outlined,
Corporations are people, a supreme new decision,
While a free people witness the loss of our vision.
Imbalanced injustice is legally executed,
Blocking light from darkness, truth can be substituted.

Occasionally, I will preface a poem with some pertinent background that may help link the personal stories of others in relation to our own experiences, feelings, and potential healing.

The story behind this next poem initially emerged to give voice to my personal experiences of injury and injustices that I perceived had been thrust upon me. How much of this recounting is subjective or objective is impossible to determine and is essentially immaterial in the end. After first writing it, I was later inspired to add a few elements that were inspired from listening to a woman share her story with me. At ninety-plus years of age, this lifelong nurse shared a story about healing she said was important to share with aspiring nursing students. This poem titled "Final Freedom" then took on a much deeper application.

She briefly described how as an adolescent, she was attacked and raped! As she ran home in shock and terror, her mother lovingly embraced her until a voice of rage emerged from her dad in the next room. Her father's quick and defensive response was that she was the "ugly duckling" of their two daughters, and if her older pretty sister never had such troubles, then certainly she must share some blame for leading someone on or contributing to this outcome in some way. That was her last attempt to ever talk to another man about that terrifying night. It certainly was not her last tearful recollection as she privately pursued healing.

Here she was, approximately eighty years later, responding to our university survey about educating the nurses of the future. Her summary focused upon the need for *listening* and *trust*, encouraging any nurse to first listen carefully and then build trust with genuine authenticity. She added that only then could healing begin to take place. She then presented me with a hand-crafted gift, letting me know in my ten years of communicating with her, she had come to trust me with this story. She also invited the dean of nursing to anonymously use her story if she felt it would helpful to other nurses with healing. Exhaling, she gently and tearfully leaned on my shoulder for one holy moment; I held her and quietly prayed for her final healing. Looking back, I believe her caring life demonstrated she had healed herself from this hurt a long time ago.

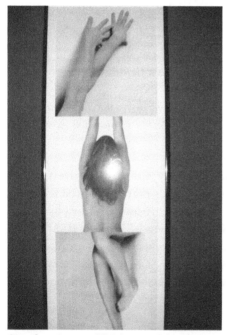

"Healing Outreach" *(Photograph by Mary Moore-Hazel)*

16

Final Freedom

Deep within, from the depths of depression,
Emotions erupt bringing forth fresh expression.
When we freely fall into a deep despair,
There surfaces a freedom, our choice to care.

As a silent but certain form of captivity,
Coerces our compliance with passivity.
It leads us to wander, so weary and lost.
Caring internally, yet outwardly tossed.

Controlling so little, if anything at all,
Having been proud, once standing so tall.
Life's walls crumble, chronically falling,
Ultimately we choose, care or withdrawing.

As fires are fanned with unthinkable hatred,
In consuming all sides, even the dead are berated.
Famished explanations, all failing to satisfy;
Only caring choices, freely given do gratify.

The freedom to speak and freely choose,
Our response to both beatings and bruise.
This final freedom, that sets us apart,
A response to pain, forgives from the heart.

Guaranteed protection, solid and secure,
Solemn and sacred, preserved and pure.
Dwelling within, it cannot to be taken,
With a will to give, were never forsaken.

This final freedom, an unalienable choice,
When under attack, a just cause to rejoice.
In acknowledging suffering, freedom is understood,
Self-healing continues, transforming bad into good.

Our final freedom, life's final verse,
As pain and loss, we cannot reverse.
Refusing to join in the hate and despair,
Hearts can heal, choosing to love and care.

Considering the incredible visionary nature of the U.S. Declaration of Independence and the U.S. Constitution, it is obvious those founding fathers distrusted any imbalance or consolidation of power as a threat to individual liberty and freedom. Despite the eighteenth-century realities of slavery and genocide of indigenous nations, this vision set forth a new course that to this day moves onward to fulfilling its universal potential for all humanity. With this resonance, the following poem emerged to honor their call to vigilance for the freedom of the human spirit.

Resisting the temptation to either romanticize or overly criticize our country's earliest grand vision of liberty, it is important to acknowledge that since the inception of the United States, our history has been mired with the usual double standards of any government. Most obvious is the fact that immigrants fleeing political and religious persecution would declare their freedom only to reestablish a society where they would utilize fear and self righteously persecute different minority populations.

The late George Carlin humorously addressed the hypocrisy of so many people searching for freedom and the tragic ways they went on to attain it for themselves at the expense of others. As of this writing, Carlin's video "America was founded on a double standard" can still be found on YouTube, offering both humor and perspective for all.

My point is not to diminish the enlightened vision of our democratic ideals, for I remain inspired and have greatly benefited from them. It is, however, meant to positively appreciate that at least some of the architects of this brilliant American document were aware that they had set in place a foundation for all peoples of the world. The genius of these documents not only demonstrated a desire to break from monarchies, despots, and oppressive religious powers, but also established a framework for fostering the spirit of real liberty and freedom. Such a structure set the stage for all to remain hopeful over time until slaves, native populations, and women (to name but a few) could all be set free as groups and individuals to live in peace as members of the greater community. Citing just a few of the most obviously suppressed and exploited groups of people in U.S. history, liberty is ever to be cherished as a work in progress.

We increasingly witness that these principles of freedom possess a universal appeal and how they increasingly resonate with hope for populations around the globe with our fellow citizens of the world.

Returning with an Act of Kindness
Releasing unanticipated forces in a patriotic act,
Unleashing ignorance spirited into action, Pushing . . .
. . . . Pounding . . .
. . . . Hounding . . .
. . . Sending sanity back into the darkest corner,
Too much smoke to see stars, or stripes,
Too dark to recognize our true colors,
Or the basic rights of so many others.
Stale illusions are freshly spun and sanitized,
Inducing a sleepwalk, by mass media-hypnotized.

Reducing personal freedoms, rebranded as patriotism,
Deducing new danger, as fear fertilizes renewed fascism.
Prying open an eyelid, so frightening at first,
We hear a calling to satisfy true liberties thirst.
As one awakens from this same old nightmare,
We shake ourselves from our sleepy stare . . .

. . . to the pulsating love always abounding . . .
. . . interdependence potentially astounding . . .
. . . freedoms spirit is forever resounding!

Free to love, to share, and care
No longer separated, or cowering in fears,
Communal healing, a breath of fresh air,
Global forgiving, can be offered to our heirs.
Refreshing, renewing, envisioning a future we share!

Earlier periods are less enlightened (perhaps arguably) than our present day. So it is that we must resist the temptation to judge past realities by today's understandings. For the purpose of encouraging potential healing for all sides of the political spectrum, the following poem was inspired to honor those who by their own free will served in the military with courageous service and a dedication to the democratic ideals of freedom and liberty. At the same time, we need to honor the many other individuals who suffered collateral injuries by the far-reaching destructive consequences of the tragedy of war.

One individual, a nurse I have known since 1970, typifies this noble intention of selfless sacrifice at great personal risk on behalf of others. A Vietnam veteran who only rarely speaks of their war experience once uttered to me about having helplessly witnessed unspeakable horrors inflicted upon fellow beings that no human should ever see or be involved in. I extend my heartfelt healing energy and empathy to all those courageous men and women who have incurred and have carried such deep battle scars. We have now come to realize that so many of our service men and women may still be dealing with PTSD and so many conflicting emotions. It is important to acknowledge that both soldier and civilian on all sides suffer from the various wounds of war!

After visiting the Vietnam Veterans Memorial in Washington, DC, in 1998, I was so moved by touching the names of former classmates on the wall that I wrote this entire poem on the one-hour flight home that day. Dedicated to everyone affected by Vietnam and all wars.

WALL OF MEMORIES

I visit the wall, walking by names so fast,
Detailing the death, in the shadows it cast.
Another war's dead, repeats another past,
The more we sent, the more lives passed.
MIAs, friendly fire, and the hostile blasts,
It should be brief, only a while would it last.
Prisoners of war, we were all shackled so slow,
Both dove and hawk, would eventually know.

Another man gone, we had viewed each frame,
The list growing long, fingering a pointless blame.
Debating the just causes with political games,
Militaries matched, who ignited these flames?
The heat of hatred casts a cold irony in stone,
Men returning berated, back home yet alone.

Neither national welcome, nor heroes paraded,
To signs of a killer, they were further degraded.
I visit the wall, walking by names so slowly,
Casting the first stone of granite seems unholy.

Each evening exposed it on the news at six,
National emotions erupted, in an explosive mix.
Parents were split as sons went off to the war,
With the sun now setting on their boy no more.

On an eve of darkness, collision and crossfire maim,
These names bear witness to both pride and shame.
I visit the wall, searching for a schoolmate's name,
Scanning those engraved, my legs now feeling lame.

A life for just a cause, at such a young age,
Frustrated families, with feelings of outrage!
Outpourings of grief, pour out into the street,
Throughout the nation, a dark hour of defeat.

Defeated by whom, and why, and what for?
By enemies abroad or ourselves on this shore?
I visit the wall as my memory replays,
Strangely renewed, finally revisiting those days!

To fight like one's fathers, helping a people in need,
Fighting for democracy, our gift of freedom indeed!
Or was it all evil, disguising some form of greed,
The imposing of wills and the sowing of bad seed?

Can history give answers for our blood and tears?
Could an answer be found after all these years?
I visited the wall despite feeling such a fear,
Still sensing a conflict, so many voices to hear.

Why did they go when it could have been me?
What might I have done, to fight or to flee?
To flee the country now, or later the jungle trail,
Remaining free on the run or at home in my jail?

Could I find a congressman, or some family connection,
To at least defer, or fully avoid such service selection?
I visit the still wall, reflecting the skies dulling haze,
Still wondering if there weren't better ways to praise.

Conscientious objections, college and a lottery did tell,
With a high number drawn, your world would be well.
If your number was not up, but that unknown other guy,
As civilians we grew weary, with another day to get by.
I visit a wall of names, wondering all of this and more,
A difference between numbers, college, class, and a war.

Sibling argued with sibling, in the ensuing national fight,
Between parents and sons, there would be no more delight.
Many mothers and fathers could not even bear to talk,
As daughters now joined in the jungles mutual stalk.

Evoking such pain renders no taming of a justified shrew,
Modern day madness, our collective Capulet versus Montague.
Drawing close to the wall, reflecting confusion and tears,
As uncivil disobedience marked our Civil War's centennial years.

On an international stage, for all the world to see,
Waging the realities of war, in exposed brutality.
Did we love them and leave them, without a chance,
Or is it all fair in love, and in the wars we romance?
I turned away from the wall, that I had come to view,
To catch my composure, still not knowing all that's true.

True or false, no leaders left to be believed?
Who murdered our president and a King?
Upon a country's conscience we still grieve,
Kennedy's killed, Martin's martyred voice still sings,
From atop the mountain, freedom's bells forever ring,
As the spirit of liberty overcomes deaths plotted sting.

In this race of arms, and political deals,
The military is blackened by race and drafting appeals.
In the streets of our nation, patience runs thin,
Our cities ablaze, over the color of skin.
Fighting at home, and over the sea,
Assassinations abounded, no leaders left to oversee.

No righteous convictions, right and left felt wrong,
Citizens sentenced to extremes, with no desire to belong.
At such a young age, we did hear of their fate,
Mirrored back home, by former students at Kent State,
Etched in their respective walls, each death we did date.
Prisoners of war, we were all shackled so slow,
Both the dove and hawk, now knew it was so.

I revisited the wall feeling nameless and alarmed,
This displaying of death, had left all of us harmed.
Recalling safe playgrounds within schoolyard gates,
Where we played games with these very classmates.
I respectfully touched, honoring their names on the wall,
They touched me back, affirming love and liberty to all.

Criminal Justice, Injustice, and Healing

In conversing with friends who have experienced the pain of incarceration, I was prompted to write about our criminal justice system and the accompanying penal codes. This is an invitation to examine their effectiveness in relation to healing and the professed desire of rehabilitation of our existing prison paradigm. In the context of this chapters focus around some of life's darker themes, I first recalled my late brother John, who was serving in the New York National Guard in 1971, when he was activated to the siege at the now infamous Attica State Prison riots in New York State. Not unlike my military veteran friends, he preferred never to talk about the tragedy except to once tell me that it was more "horror" than he could ever witness again. He was admittedly quite jaded from the experience and said he had grown to have more empathy for prisoners and acquired a healthy skepticism concerning the policing authorities of our world as public protectors. Simply accepting his feelings as a participant and eyewitness, it gives one pause to seek new perspective on this aspect of human healing for both victims and perpetrators, be it the prosecuted or law enforcement.

Whether one has been summoned to jury duty, has been accused of a crime, or is seeking to address an injustice where we have been violated in some way, our criminal justice systems affect all of us over our lifetime. Along with political appeals for law and order, there also exists a growing concern over the ever escalating number of new laws, the resulting backlog of litigations, and the increased incidence of police force, growing incarceration replete with an expansion of newly privatization prison construction. Prisons for profit?

Pausing to gain some perspective on the penal paradigms of our present justice system, it needs to be acknowledged that our present system was in fact a positive historical step forward from the often brutal practices of ancient Rome, medieval justice, church-sponsored inquisitions, or recent twentieth-century dictatorships. As is well documented, in these models, one's guilt or innocence was left to the savage whims of those few holding unbridled power. By merely seeking perspective, we are freed to explore if these issues may be ready for further evolving some two hundred-plus years since their most modern conception. Will rapidly changing times give us insight into discovering and creating possible improvements that could produce more positive results, ranging from our disturbing statistics of increased crime and an expanding population of incarcerated citizens?

My own involvements have included personally testifying as a victim to identify a serial burglar who I found entering my home, being in a jury pool to potentially serve on a rape case, and attending court proceedings in moral support of friends accused of various offenses. I was left with heartfelt and conflicting feelings around these sobering realities. These circumstances all speak to how we treat each other, and regardless of who cast the first stone, the truth is we all pay a penalty for the mistreatment of each other. This is true regardless if we are personally victimized by a crime, if we serve on a jury, or if we are convicted and punished for breaking a law.

With a new dialogue, perhaps we can continue discovering progressive new approaches with better outcomes over previous retribution and punishment codes. New practices may further free us from the prisons of our historical past, which we are not condemned to repeat. The question is can we improve our desired results by reversing crime and reducing the growing cost of imprisoning so many of our fellow citizens?

The ideals of our society challenge us to endeavor to improve upon reducing crime and any maltreatment and violation of each other. In this, we all have a mutual stake in advancing liberty and justice for all.

As free people, it is always up to us! There is great need for healing around this topic, healing for all parties, from perpetrator to police officer. From these experiences, I composed the following poem to encourage a renewed reflection upon how we view *justice* and create yet new foundations to promote more freedom.

Richard Francis Moore

The Continuing Ballad of Reading Jail*

In Oscar's wildest of dreams,
He hoped we'd hear silenced screams,
Unfairly burdened by a one sided trial,
Only forgiveness frees, to grant survival.

Witness water boarding in Guantanamo,
Observe our uncivil muting of Geronimo.
Bar by bar, we lay bricks upon bricks,
Increasing the rate of criminal verdicts.

In the midst of so many righteous convictions,
Fearfully forfeiting our most ideal depictions,
Our laws restrict more freedoms and rights,
Will life and liberty become lost in plain sight?

*This poem was inspired as an update to Oscar Wilde's poem, "The Ballad of Reading Gaol," written in 1897.

Prisoners of our own Making

Cracking down on crime, it is black and white,
We have a lock on toughness, of wrong and right.
An odd sort of pride in being number one all the time,
Resulting in a byproduct of the imprisoning kind.

In kind we serve up multiple terms,
Yet with no thought of binding term limits,
A resourceful politic, and self-serving vote,
Not a thought of everyone's own contribution,
God forbid forgiveness, as we increase retribution.

An escalating procession of terminal sentences for the living.
The living dead run free, imprisoned by fearful thinking.
Imbalanced judgment can tip the scales of justices,
Courting a future of some supreme injustice.

A production of prisons greases the systems gears,
As the fear of fear bars harmony from our ears.
The seeds of discontent are indeed unkind,
An unnatural growth, of the criminal mind,
Malcontent ingredients brew this new breed,
Penal cells increase with a cancerous speed.

Mostly men in fact, yet a growing minority of men,
More menacing than any original skin,
Akin to a black mark on our cultural condition,
As highway robbery paves the road to perdition.

Upon this rough road, where will it lead, pray tell?
Will it be lined with chain gangs, marking a road to hell?
Yet we are not condemned to any singular road,
We may exit anytime, off this dreary death row.

Good growth may lead us to beautiful destinations,
Rerouting a course for our own heart's salvation.
So how can we ever free ourselves,
From constructing more terrifying cells?

If humanity is ever going to really break free,
Of incarcerating a growing segment of society,
We must be part of a solution more visionary.
We are the key to unlocking freedom and liberty.

A cornerstone paradigm of our culture is a commitment to a free-market economy, consciously linked to our liberty and pursuit of happiness. Our history of capitalism documents many rapid and beneficial developments for humankind, especially during the Industrial Revolution. This history also captures the financial evolution of corporate-owned coal mining towns, labor exploitation, unsafe labor conditions, child labor, the Great Depression, and the more recent scandals resulting in tax payer bailouts of our financial institutions, replete with Ponzi schemes, mortgage scandals, and trading violations. A great deal of popular opinion (from both the right and the left) continues to ferment around a growing lack of faith in a system periodically experiencing economic depressions and needing to be artificially propped up with outright corporate welfare at taxpayer expense.

At the same time, entrenched CEOs are rewarded with bonuses for their business "leadership." Writing about these subjects tempts the most positive of individuals to become wary, if not outright disillusioned regarding these markets needing oversight before it all repeats itself. While I am not a cynic, I find it a positive and courageous act to discuss real results and where we may be headed as a society and a world.

The credibility crises with our present financial systems grows worldwide as citizens already feel it has been fractured. If populations continue losing faith in unmonitored capitalism, one wonders if a new economic system may evolve this century. Perhaps some new paradigm or hybrid system might create a more comprehensive economy, one in which more individuals are personally invested in contributing to a mutually beneficial world economy with stable and sustainable societies. Can the values of free enterprise be effectively integrated with a genuine element of social responsibility?

I have personally experienced painful financial losses through questionable management of my IRA investments that ranged from excessive trading for commissions to my poor judgment of once investing in what turned out to be a classic Ponzi scheme. While some of these fraudulent individuals were eventually jailed, like most investors, my funds went largely unrecovered. These setbacks do not even begin to address the ramifications of the economic collapse of 2008. Fortunately, I learned my lesson and ceased responding to offers that seemed too good to be true. Fortunately, I never bet the farm, but I did lose valued savings for my children's college tuition.

In the end, I am still blessed to have the roof over my head. Many were not so lucky, as witnessed by increasing homeless populations. I wrote the following poetic trilogy on behalf of millions of individuals more adversely affected than I was. It addresses many other stories that other investors shared with me on what we might term the *ultimate illusion of security* in our world, be it economic, political, military, social, or otherwise.

A Security Trilogy
(Insecurity)

(I) Lock, Stock, and Barrel

Capitalist collusion yields an economic free fall
Scheming an enterprising free for all,
Red ink graffiti on that street of discolored walls,
The bell now tolls, as another crash befalls.

We are never forewarned,
Of these economic hair brained storms,
Repeating crazy cycles so unwise,
As insiders openly orchestrate to monopolize.
Incapable of resisting their compulsive greed,
Chain letters bait investors, phishing dishonest deeds.

Capitalism crashes, but not from socialists in the street,
But from white collar thieves, whom foreign bankers greet.
No oversight from a White House or congressional acts,
Leaving CEOs to their devices, a bonus for fiscal attacks.

Capitalist cannibals toll their closing bell,
But the bell tolls for all, as markets freely fell.
Still dressed for drinking, in pin striped apparel,
With financials failing, losing lock stock and barrel.

(Security Lapse)

(II) Sad Sack of Cash

Enough of all the political guys,
Or bankrupt bankers in dignified disguise,
As illusions abound in all this strife,
Only distracting us from our spirit's real life.

Robbing us daily of joy and peace,
Taxing patience and pocket, piece by piece.
Focused upon the thefts on Wall Street,
Not even subtle, not even discreet.

Collusion and corruption, fail us so complete,
Free enterprise sows a free fall on Wall Street.
Brief cases conceal computer chips and cash,
In races overseas to transfer their secret stash.
A greedy feeding frenzy is nearly complete,
Free market corrections, yield grand theft deceit.

Fugitive CEOs are ironically killing capitalism,
More effective than Marxists, who marched for socialism.
Incapable of resisting their repetitive greed
Fleecing their investors, with each phony deed.
Hedging their security, they sowed bad seed,
To a growing insecurity, they are guilty indeed.

Correctional facilities provide a suitable pinstripe,
Broken brokers roll up sleeves, for their tears to wipe.
From cell phone to cell window, within walled streets,
Selling schemes, begs reform for all of U.S. to meet.

(Secured Back in the Black)

(III) Taking Stock in Your Security

So much for all the hard work and saving,
It appears we worked under a modern enslaving.
Hard to believe white collar crime is so brash,
Manufacturing yet another marketed crash!

Once we labored, over obstacles braving,
Again indentured, from cradle to graving.
From faith in the future, in error believing,
Refinancing our lives, with heirs left grieving.

Back into the black, into that which is real,
Invest in a precious gem, a piece they cannot steal.

So take stock in what is really of worth,
Of family and friends, and a new birth.
So I send you greetings beyond the news,
Of lasting friendships, and loving views.

30

Back into the black, where intuition can feel,
Investing within, a peace no one can steal.

Deep within, where peace is quietly spoken,
Our worth is secured beyond coin or token,
Beyond the surface lies true vision and sight,
Securing our growth, yields lasting delight.

Our soul soars above what seems black and white,
Assessing our wealth measured by love and light.

Chapter 1 ends its varied examination of cross sections
of our modern life and concludes with a retrospective
poem on this theme of declaring independence.

Engendered Debts
(Guaranteed Risks)

Caught in the midst of a common confusion,
Comes an insight of unexpected infusion.
Adding new ingredients into the human mix,
Sums up solutions, for problems to fix.

A check and balance is missing in the male,
Historically discounting the valued female,
Auditing a paternal error of devaluation,
We shortchanged citizens in every nation,
Multiplying problems with masculine division,
Equates to a divided world, in need of revision.

A lesson in the form of Adam's separation,
Attempting to blame our Eve of destruction.

A-bomb reduces the value of humanity,
A guaranteed bottom line of a patriarchy!

Crashes and corruption is the word on the street,
As our world's capitals continue to compete,
In ordering some missile-led, capital sentence,
Stockpiles will fall, before the ashes of repentance.
With a bull market's manipulated starts,
We degrade the value of the sum of our parts.

Hedged in the sale of this Adam, the sun did set on every Eve,
Yet the dawning of the goddess, offers interest in reprieve.
Reprimanding the righteous, who scare and deceive,
Projecting grim illusions, women can mercifully relieve.

The number of times we may stumble or reel,
Can add to our growth, if we but choose to heal.
For within the depths of a man and woman's heart,
We sense our power to create a fresh start.

Yes our loving future is always assured,
We are all protected, and divinely insured.
Recreating is inherent, in our essential DNA,
Despite many big bangs, we are all here stay.

Such are the crossroads, as we create new history,
Observing the common bonds of all humanity.
Formed in God's image, in love we are set free,
With abundant resources from sea to shining sea.
So in your travels, go forth in love and in liberty,
Encircle the world, embracing love globally.

Forgiving engendered debts, profits are guaranteed,
Beyond stacked decks, once dominated by greed.
A new fusion of human thought, refusing an old lie,
This truth we have sought, on love's foundation we rely.
Revealing all falsehood, exposing the illusions we see,
Engendering the meaning of life, we can declare our liberty!

Reflections for Healing
(Optional Journal)

Chapter 1

In the Darkness of Illusions
Understanding First Exposures

What observations may have caught your attention or further interest in chapter 1?

Did you gain any insight or understanding(s) in regard to the various topics in this chapter?

Can you identify any societal paradigms that serve as a foundation of human civilization?
Positive?

Negative?

Did any poetic mediation prove insightful or helpful in any way?

Your Other Notes:

Chapter 2

Early in the Journey

Understanding the Silence

Looking back upon my early adulthood, it might best be described as an experience containing a learning curve in my ability to better communicate both internally and externally. Here I recall various lessons in listening before speaking. While not always a pretty process, it often appears that our personal growth is linked to our understanding subtle "sounds of silence" that quietly resonate within our spirits. One definition of silence in Webster's dictionary is it is simply the "absence of mention, or sound, or noise." In relation to hurt and healing, this chapter expresses a fusion of many quiet influences upon me during my early adult years.

Typical of many people, much of my young adulthood contained a certain baptism by fire quality to it. Given the lack of experience that accompanies our youth, this maturation period has been humorously described as "fake it until you make it." By appreciating and gracefully embracing this natural growth process, it can equip us to better address healing opportunities throughout our life. With an ear to understanding how different forms of silence can influence our world in extremely different ways, we begin by examining various aspects of silence. By understanding various forms of quiet ranging from a fearful destructive silence to an enlightening meditative silence we may find a healthy balance that resonates with increasing frequency. Three reflections for understanding silence are explored in the following contexts:

- Contrasts externally imposed and internally passive silence
- Perspectives on the quiet silence within oneself
- Quiet revelations

1. Observe externally imposed and internally passive silence: What was left unspoken?

It seems only natural that most of us experience a difficult time discerning the purpose or direction early in our life's journey. It is generally challenging for us to articulate and speak of who we think we are at a young age. With limited life experience, it is improbable that in our formative years, we could effectively give physical voice to our deeper purpose and say where we might desire to go and which roads we will need to take to get there.

Just as we once grew awkwardly into adolescence, we recall that we invariably increased in our strength, grace, and beauty as we moved into adulthood. Always present along the way is a deeply seeded spiritual dimension quietly calling us to go within to nurture and explore our unique potential for personal growth. Despite this inaudible inner calling, it can seem at times pathetic—even pitiful—that because of the many loud and conflicting external influences, we fail to hear or listen to this inner voice. We may choose to compliantly proceed in life by mimicking generational conditioning of what is expected of us. In this space, we tend to hold back our own expressiveness and opinions and may even repress our emotions and creativity.

At the very least, we tend to mute our honest critical feelings, and perhaps even worse, we might hesitate to speak sweet things to each other. Sharing our sweetness and goodwill is a gift we all possess and deserve to softly speak in beneficially hearing from each other! So why do we tend to suppress the expression of our heartfelt feelings and thoughts in our world as we grow throughout the distinct stages of our life?

Is our silence born out of some ego-centered defense mechanism such as a simple fear of rejection? For whatever reasons, it appears that we can turn a deaf ear to each other while at the same time justify muting our voices. Sustained silence can have a contagious effect on us by conveying a dysfunction of indifference, as if biting our tongues long term may also negatively affect our vocal chords. Regardless of any explanation, it is apparent from my observations that a dulling of our senses can occur during difficult emotional times if we chronically suffer in silence.

What then do these muted feelings possibly have to tell us? Do these behaviors have anything to tell us now? Might other reasons include an unfamiliarity or outright disbelief in the concept of unconditional love? As a divine concept, it may seem just too good or utopian for us to believe in and consequently not worth trying to articulate. It is quite conceivable that this concept of being unconditionally loved is so totally foreign to one's life experience that it cannot be grasped let alone trusted. Sadly, most have experienced love's betrayal which can result in making it difficult to risk trusting again in the promise of another loving relationship.

Perhaps we all carry with us a chronic anxiety from times when we felt misunderstood or unloved. Additionally, we are also confronted with societal norms that promote often confusing concepts around romantic love that can mislead us into obsessive and possessive behaviors that are actually the antithesis of love. We may behave by attaching to, latching onto, and unintentionally even try to possess one another in the name of love. Here our love can become an equally harmful obsession. Simultaneously, we fear even small perceived rejections will compound our burdens from previous disappointments. The resulting escalation of insecurities can condition us to feelings of unworthiness and just not being lovable. Left unchecked, such frigid feelings can silently transform into a self-imposed solitary confinement. Conversely, it is important to know that silence can be used as a positive force if we use it to observe these feelings and behavioral patterns. If we become aware of these realities, we can free ourselves from harmful cycles!

Maybe we fail to speak up because fear we will not be heard. This adds to our perceptions of feeling invisible and isolated amid bright lights and loud noises of flashy personalities lauded in a world that markets exaggerated imagery. In other instances, it can just be a case of pent-up frustration from past efforts to successfully communicate, where we dared to courageously share our feelings only to have them go unregistered in another's unreceptive mind. Differing from rejection, it is simply not being listened to or heard. This sting of indifference can hurt and can also make us feel unworthy and can ultimately leave us feeling uncertain of all our previous efforts to foster relationships of any kind. One could understandably be left concluding that communicating with our fellow beings is just not worth all the bother.

Under the increased weight of these painful experiences, we may resign ourselves to accept the negative presumption that we will continue to remain largely unseen and unheard in any substantive manner by our fellow beings. With lowered expectations safely in place as a defense mechanism, one cautiously moves onward—onward perhaps, but not necessarily forward. This common behavioral reaction tempts us along the way, but this apparent safety net can become an entangling trap. It can leave us tied up in knots with a frustrated existence as we remain in a fixed position while others drift dangerously away and out of our reach. In a sense, we can unwittingly manifest these unwanted experiences and produce the proverbial self-fulfilling prophecy of creating what we fear the most and desire the least. In this example, we may live with a sense of being alone. It is this sense of separation or being alone either physically, mentally, emotionally, psychologically, or even spiritually that leads to much illness. Conversely, extreme isolation can trigger us into constructive action as we reawaken to again reach outward to others and endeavor to reconnect for some much needed healing.

Even exceptionally gifted geniuses and enlightened beings have historically reported suffering from a sense of isolation, but perhaps for different reasons. In their own growth process, they have expressed painful frustration from their heightened awareness of the desolate emotional, intellectual, and spiritual landscape prevailing around the globe at their particular time in human history. Be it the Buddha, Jesus, Da Vinci, Galileo, Michelangelo, or Einstein, examples abound of historically gifted leaders and individuals that were isolated by a prevailing ignorance. The well-known biblical phrase "Forgive them, for they know not what they do" speaks volumes for our recognizing that this obvious lack of awareness serves as a key in pointing us in the direction of healing via forgiveness until individual and global awareness increases to an eventual tipping point. Recognizing such repetitive historical cycles actually speaks to unspoken yearnings as a sort of emotional black hole that attempts to suck us into the silent darkness. At one time or another, we may all ask ourselves, "Should I once again risk new efforts at genuinely communicating with others despite failures of past experiences with my fellow beings?" Understandably, we might utilize our free will to continue remaining quiet.

There is another aspect of silence in our modern world that escalates at an alarming pace given our pathological history of chronic war. Human history seems to quietly accept its well chronicled documentation of never-ending wars around the globe. Such escalating destruction is leading us to the brink of self-destruction. It is an invitation to either a new dark age for the human spirit or the annihilation of the species. All of this continues amid the contrasting advancements of our sacred scientific temples and the marvelous technologies of our *progressive* times. This paradox of human progress alongside the realistic potential for a self-destructive Armageddon is incomprehensible and mutually incompatible. This modern rhythm we march to is not one of our heart's rhythmic beatings. It is the drumbeat of discordant and distracting sounds from the mind of man. The careening sounds of man-made machinery contain escalating decibel levels whose sheer volume creates a different form of deafness. This cacophony of chronically generated noise eliminates the positive natural quiet from our spaces and souls, drowning out the sweet sounds of birds singing, while televisions mesmerize us from recognizing those faces in our very presence. Think of the nature of *quiet* being akin to good and bad cholesterol. There exist both an inspirational quiet and a dysfunctional quiet, and our health depends on finding a balance.

Despite increased global literacy and excellent electronic communications in our modern world, in some ways, we may actually be communicating less effectively in spirit than our ancestors in the Dark Ages. Consider the way the ancients could see the heavens in the dark sky with great clarity with an easy upward glance, and then listen to each other's observations around a community campfire. While not attempting to romanticize the Dark Ages, today we admittedly must travel to remote regions of the planet to avoid the interference of our world's bright lights to view our same Milky Way Galaxy. Our auditory senses are bombarded by so much noisy background of traffic, news, music, while our vision for the world is dulled, and our minds are distracted by a seemingly excessive need for entertainment.

At least at an individual level, we might consider occasionally shifting our engines into neutral and slow down the extreme vibrations for a sacred moment in time. By quietly pausing a bit, we might be able to hear each other (or our own self) at a deeper level. Whether you call it spirit, soul, emotion, intellect, or any expression you choose, at this time, we must truly begin to earnestly communicate with each other and, more importantly, to understand one another. Six billion unique people cannot and need not agree, but we can all seek to understand each other! This will require quietly listening before speaking thoughtfully. As we journey through life, this aspect of silence can play a great role in healing, as we do not want to fail to speak our contribution to our fellow beings. This is a subtle but significant paradigm shift that we can create on the horizon, and may we not leave our words unspoken.

2. Perspectives on the quiet silence within:

In your own private and individual quiet moments, have you ever received inspired thoughts or solutions or in any way heard the mystical or divine speaking softly to you?
Shhh . . . Listen . . .

Toward that end, I suggest that on occasion, everyone should consider pursuing an experience of finding a truly isolated and quiet space. I had once sought out time to travel deep into the Nevada desert, and I later took another opportunity to explore the Rocky Mountains off the usual paths. It was in the desert where I accidentally discovered the deepest quiet space, both physically and spiritually. Here, for the first time, I experienced the absence of sound in pure silence.

During those days in such remote and extremely isolated locations, it was as if I were in a vacuum, not hearing so much as a bird's call or even a whispered breeze in my ear! Nothing! It felt strange and uncomfortable, yet it was powerfully peaceful and calming as I sat in stillness for hours. In this physical and silent stillness, I was deeply moved. At times, I was lonely, and other times, the surreal experience caused me to laugh out loud, again drawing my attention to the surrounding vacuum like atmosphere. In a trancelike state, my spirit outwardly offered inaudible prayers while absorbing inspired insights on our human and divine connection with mystical clarity . . . beyond words . . .

One of my funnier observations that day was when it occurred to me that as one of nine children, I shared a bedroom with as many as five brothers at once. This environment offered only the rarest moments of silence during my early life. Many years later, on my honeymoon, I actually commented to my bride how quiet it was at night with only the two of us in the room. I find it very funny that I have come to be writing about aspects of silence.

Given my own noisy history, I fully appreciate that modern day circumstances can make it very difficult for us to find such quiet spaces in daily life. I would nevertheless exhort everyone to pursue extreme silence at least occasionally. At the very least, try to get as far away from the roads and activity you possibly can. When you seek and find such silence, you may feel it deeply as I did, as a strange and somewhat staggering void. As I mentioned, my experience was at first an uncomfortable sensation, or lack of sensation might be a better expression. In this silence, our soul may at last listen as our spirits can now begin to softly speak to us from deep within our being, not unlike the ancients gazing into the starry night sky.

Again, if you cannot presently pursue this ideal circumstance, try your best to seek out some measure of quiet space and time for visiting your inner self. This may require pragmatic innovations such as using ear plugs in your most private available room, maybe at three o'clock in the morning, but know you will likely find it worthwhile once you get past the initial strangeness of being silent together with your inner spirit, and discover your deeper self! As you ease into your quiet internal space, listen close, for in time, it can begin to be both comforting and comfortable. Silence has the potential to yield inspirations on life's deepest mysteries and truths! Here your heart can hear messages it has been holding for you, resonating beyond words to remind you of what your spirit/inner self/true identity has always known. Yes, each of us possesses an identity beyond our inherited birth labels, holding our own unique destiny with new answers to old questions and creative solutions to ancient problems.

The various dimensions of silence can help positively penetrate whatever our current circumstances may be at the moment, so try and resist waiting for the perfect environment to begin setting aside your quiet times alone. These less-than-ideal situations should motivate us to create some time for quietly listening, which can help slowly liberate our tongue-tied moments to more articulately speak and share our own truth. By more freely expressing our purpose (not insensitively or recklessly), we can also affirm our inherent connection together. If done authentically, we will all further free ourselves and our cultures, institutions, traditions, and families from any shallow pretenses that can partition and limit us. Genuine and fresh communications will help us replace any past paradigms that may have been constructed upon historical falsehoods before they collapse upon us.

The escalating stress of present-day circumstances on institutional structures within our respective cultures could entrap us in even more trouble if we permit it to continue as it has. If we are not careful, our prevailing environment of global conflicts will increasingly yield unnecessary destruction that exponentially grows from our paradigms portraying an artificial sense of human separation. Poor communications or the proverbial silent treatment directed toward our fellow beings will not benefit anyone's situation. The time to talk as a human family has arrived, and with the technological capabilities for global communications, it realistically does provide us with a most positive opportunity for unprecedented beneficial outcomes.

I am happy to say that it increasingly appears to me that more and more individuals worldwide are communicating with an increasing awareness of humanities' multifaceted connections. Human consciousness, when combined with these electronic communications, can be miraculous in relation to this emerging capability to connect us in so many ways. In this light, our fellow beings are now increasingly daring to express themselves to us with refreshing droplets of authentic insight. Picture these drops rippling outward as they expansively spread a healthy respect for each other, streaming into the living rivers of our lives that flow into the collective oceans we share in common. Such currents begin drawing us back together to create powerful new waves resonating with our extraordinary shared destiny. Understanding this, let us make a joyful noise by giving voice to what unites us, quietly pause and listen to the resulting sound waves echo our resounding connection around the world and the entire universe. Such is the vibration humanity is destined to move into.

In any attempt to more fully comprehend our uncommon union as sons and daughters of creation, we must first individually choose to dive into our pooled divinity. By carefully listening to each other before speaking, we may move humankind forward. In proceeding, we can sense we are being intuitively drawn closer to the life-giving waters of a celestial and baptismal remembrance of a singular origin as a human race. Forget the need for theological, philosophical debates, as the obvious mathematical perfection and synchronicity of the universe is a powerfully miraculous testimony in any language or tradition.

In primal waves, we hear the waters breaking the silence, perhaps reminding us of a universal calling to remember we are on a true loving journey, entering a new awareness of the joy of *just being*! If our distant memory of one origin is but recognized and remembered, there would no longer be any reason for any further postponement of expressing our all-loving nature. Acknowledging humanity's background of historical separation and conflict, our quiet spaces of meditative silence offer us the opportunity for the remembrance and revelation of our mutual salvation and healing for one and all who so choose.

Continuing these thoughts with a different image, emblematic of creating our elusive salvation was that "giant leap for mankind" in 1969, marked by the first lunar landing. Astronauts looked down upon planet earth with a borderless global perspective, helping humans see this orb as a glowing opportunity. Daring to take those first brave steps into this new sea of tranquility, we have always been guided by the pull of the moon's tides and the light that so beneficially reflects upon our world. As part of everyone's personal individual journey, we each must decide to courageously step into these tidal currents of our collective world. Observing with new vision, our perspective of global oneness is further evolving at this moment in human history.

In this context, it is noteworthy that most religious and spiritual traditions still express a long overdue hope for peace and a brotherhood/sisterhood in reuniting our entire human family. This is true despite the tragic and flagrant contradictions of history recording so many ungodly wars and self-righteous intolerance in the name of religion This litany of religious conflicts has tarnished the professed loving intentions of the world's religions, significantly sacrificing their integrity and trust. Yet now is a new time, a new opportunity for us and our countries, cultures, and institutions (secular and religious) to reform old concepts of separation and update our foundations for building upon our common purpose together.

Leaving history behind us for the moment, it is tempting to just leapfrog over the tough realities of the modern times and circumstances we share today. It is, however, essential to acknowledge the many challenges within the current paradigms of our world powers at this time. In addressing individual and societal healing, I have watched how healing and social change often occurs independently outside of society's most powerful structures as these institutions usually end up functioning to preserve an often unhealthy status quo. Indeed, history does document that substantive change is most often initiated outside of our mainstream power structures. Whether it is a case for civil rights, women's rights, or even alternative health therapies, change usually happens when great numbers of individuals become consciously aware of the need to act.

Beyond simply observing any flawed foundations in our human institutions, we are now empowered to acknowledge and openly discuss these deficiencies without wasting any energy on who is to blame for any shortcomings, for ultimately, we all share in the glory or the shame of our outcomes, each of us with opportunities to exacerbate the problem or aid in solutions. It may be increasingly accurate to refer to the world's institutional powers as being increasingly powerless in respect to reigning in war and relieving the pervasive poverty of our present-day circumstances. For the moment, our structures appear impotent in reversing growing greed and corresponding human suffering, beginning with the basic daily needs of food, water, clothing, and shelter for billions of people around the planet.

As our present paradigms continue failing to recognize the true nature of our shared origin, they unwittingly justify more war and separation ranging from nationality, economics, and religious sectarianism. This simply limits our ability to grasp the ultimate understanding of our connectivity with one another and continues the ongoing path of destruction now under way. My point regarding the ineffectiveness of our institutions is not to focus on criticism, nor does it represent any cynical conclusions. On the contrary, it is positively shared as a candid observation citing such basic plagues as war, homelessness, hunger, disease, energy, and pollution continue to pick up speed and scourge us with their repetitive cycles. As I have stated, we all share in this moment of opportunity for new paradigm shifts. By honestly acknowledging this growing calamity it poses the age old question: Why do we expect new results by using old remedies that have not produced positive results in the past?

Can the vantage point of those on the international space station help us better see our way to new paths, new remedies and results? Based on the experiences of my own journey, I believe that our legitimate hopes and realistic sense of true optimism in the future resides in each individual's innate creative power. I believe that such implanted power resides individually within us. By contrasting individual versus institutional power, it can reaffirm the old adage that politicians are indeed only a mirror of the populace. Historic change as we have noted often takes place when a critical mass of the populace makes their convictions and insights publicly known. When this shift occurs in enough individuals, those holding positions of power can then *feel safe* in making the necessary societal changes in their respective institutions.

So it is we cannot simply sit back and blame institutions and those in authority because they will only initiate substantive change when enough citizens passionately encourage those changes. Remember we give individuals authority, be it an act of commission in voting or omission in our silence in the face of suffering. Be assured that leaders will ultimately respond to needed changes, otherwise, face the inevitable fate of pharaohs, emperors, kings, dictators, presidents, prime ministers, popes, and yes, even corporate CEOs. Remember this is not to vilify anyone but a reminder that in the final analysis we all share responsibility for final outcomes.

As of this writing early in the twenty-first century, we approach an historical crossroads as citizens feel increasingly insecure as traditional institutions show stress fractures, along with the fraying old paradigms. Politicians and other leaders desperately search to find safety from their electorate as new viewpoints give birth to fresh paradigms for the next generation of civilization. Born from the trauma of turbulent change, citizens will construct new foundations with politicians slowly following behind until feeling safe enough to claim these initiatives for change as their own ideas to champion.

American civil rights offer a great example of this dynamic. In the 1950s, very few political leaders felt enough popular support to risk their own careers by changing the status quo. Yet just ten years later, enough public awareness and pressure existed for elected officials to dare moving society beyond previously held understandings that had so brutally limited the individual freedoms of various minority groups. Other twentieth-century examples include Mahatma Gandhi's exceptional leadership that inspired and empowered so many citizens to courageously express themselves and ultimately free them from the unsustainable paradigm of colonial rule. Similarly, the contributions of many courageous leaders of the women's suffragette movement cannot be overstated in expanding freedom and liberty for the whole of humankind. Despite the progress over the last century, the ongoing imbalance of female leadership in our world continues to reflect a deeply rooted lack of understanding and an unhealthy imbalance between the genders. This remains an ongoing concern for nurturing the health of our world.

These examples can help us understand that such tipping points for change in human history can only occur when individual consciousness reaches a critical threshold that the collective whole can be positively utilized to help move all of us forward. Such cooperative concepts are captured well in the American Declaration of Independence and a constitution emphasizing the balance of power and a vigilant responsibility of a citizenry that is critical to individual liberty. This is where people might sense a realistic reason for optimism. As one comes to understand, these historic shifts in our progress originate not from one leader but, ultimately, from many individuals taking responsibility for their thoughts, actions, and beliefs.

As citizens become aware of being individually responsible for the beliefs and actions of the organizations and groups to whom they belong (e.g., social group, church, political party, etc.), change occurs naturally from within these groups. Only then can *we the people* continue to cocreate and fulfill the greater promise of our independent declaration and live out the creed that we are indeed created equal. After all, we now realize our Declaration of Independence contained a visionary intention as is demonstrated with the eventual abolition of slavery and child labor laws and the granting of women's rights.

When we look back, it is easier to see how the human desire for liberty and freedom is a universal desire, and it continues to evolve from a time when most of these freedoms were far from a reality. It is a reminder that free speech is a cherished value, and in terms of our focus on understanding various aspects of silence, it reminds us of our responsibility to first listen to other viewpoints and only then respectfully speak our truth thoughtfully and truthfully.

Now let us now briefly examine this dynamic of silence from our third and final vantage point.

3. Quiet revelations: Healing our world begins with individual introspection before rippling outwardly to others.

Harkening back to my primary school years, I will forever remember a positive mantra the nuns routinely affirmed. Advising us to understand that we were born with two ears and two eyes but only one mouth with which to speak, they emphasized a lesson that we should remember to look twice (to observe) and listen twofold (to understand) before carefully considering what we might speak or not. Predictably, they followed with instruction to always speak the truth. This chapter on silence is ultimately about communications, verbal and non-verbal, and how they can hurt or heal any and all of us.

In this spirit, these writings are never intended to cast any judgment or to fault any one institution or individual. In this context, we can be better prepared to proceed without defensiveness, increasing our ability to benefit from the view of hindsight. Knowing that these observations of the past need not condemn anyone, we can remain focused on our sole purpose, which is only to assist healing by clinically comprehending other versions of history and other accounts of reality. Here we benefit from new perspectives while respecting the legitimate feelings of many diverse viewpoints, including a healthy review of our personal beliefs to date. Careful listening to such opposing points of view can lead us to greater understanding since one person's truth does not discount or discard another person's experience of an equally opposite truth.

You need not agree with another, but to truly understand another position is critical to living together and thus creating a healthier future for all. (For example, scientifically documenting the critical value of the North Pole does not devalue or invalidate the significance of the South Pole in supporting our planet and the resulting balance of life all over the globe. Our temperate climates could not exist without our poles in place!) In plain English, polar opposites mutually support a healthy future for many cultures. Opposite beliefs need not serve as conflicting forces.

Our own healing and personal power can also help assist the collective health of all. This understanding could help shift our world in important new directions that could personally benefit oneself and all of humanity in the generations that follow us. Some obvious applications include defusing long-standing religious and sectarian differences, military conflicts, or even legislative stalemates and stagnation still so predominant in the early twenty-first century.

Again these writings, stories, and poems do not represent to advance some idealism or any preferred new religious, political, or philosophical movement. They are actually offered as pragmatic observations with practical thoughts that should appeal equally to the artist, academic, scientist, spiritualist, politician, religious leader, along with the professed agnostic and atheist alike. Their meaning is more effective when read with a sense of openness to understand new perspectives even if you may not agree. Here lies the hope for new and positive solutions, for it is in our silent reflections and meditations where we first begin healing ourselves. Equipped with greater understanding and balance, we will be able to more calmly speak our truth openly to the world without fanning hatred or further hostility. By reestablishing speaking in respectful tones, we will begin to free ourselves to begin sharing our collective and sacred wisdom together and begin our healing together.

Chapter 2 concludes with the previously stated format of speaking to the heart with some poetic reflections related to the silence of my own early journey. All of these poems were born from the conflicting circumstances described around the themes of communication throughout this chapter, and are here to support the healing of many common human conditions. As this is a personal process, only you will determine if these poetic meditations resonate in your own life experience or in relation to any groups you were either born into (e.g., culture, religion, or country), including any other values you have previously held that may speak to your heart now. May we journey onward to thoughtfully speak our hearts truth in a spirit of increasing communion together.

Photo courtesy of Maya Yonika

PARADOXICAL QUERY

The desire to focus, and better see,
Beyond our heartbeat, the meaning to be.
Are answers simple to our complexity?

Creatures from heaven, humankind fell?
From within and without, demons from hell?
Is existential madness, tolling our soul's bell?

Are we basically bad, or inherently good?
Duality debated; both were staggered but withstood,
Our spins become blurred, and misunderstood.

History has witnessed, the brutal and mean,
While the good and heroic, have also been seen.
How do we reconcile; what does this all mean?

Life is often so nice, but also harsh and short,
Words can't explain, the deep hurt we report.
Should we believe the bad, or to the good resort?

A spectacular show, sunrise in the morning,
Later day fears, of a sudden storm warning.
Who will be next, for our mutual mourning?

Accounting for good, can't discount our pain,
Can the human spirit credit suffering to our gain?
Can we embrace both, or must one we disdain?

The silence of death, the starkness of loss,
Deep seas without breath, in darkness lost.
Is their rhyme or reason, salvation at such a cost?

Fire and flood, emit emotions so rife,
Death spawns an apprehension to life.
Will a shot of love penetrate the strife?

In the eye of these storms, our vision clears,
As a cool calming, silences calamity and fear,
Warmly recalling what we hold precious and dear!

As darkness subsides, the light no longer dim,
Rejecting this reaper, and to all that is grim.
Returning from gloom, to a quiet peace within,
Surrendering a smile, granting a grin.

Cryptic Communication
"snoitacinummoc citpyrc"

You know the type, typically with so many faces to show,
Stereotypically in triplicate, of mind, body, and soul.
Rehearsed rhetoric, orchestrating opposite poles,
Constructing class warfare, creating false roles.
Genuine communication is our right to protect,
Does it assault honesty to be "politically correct"?
True communication, a spontaneous heartfelt expression,
Sacrificed and skewed by labels disguising suppression.
A forthright phrase, must be publicly corrected,
By political agendas, buying the elite we elected.

Whatever is now vogue, and is currently in fashion,
Inclusion with intolerance, remains of old blind passion.
From well-intentioned intellects, and utopian dreams,
Flow evolving extremists, espousing emotional schemes.

Required reconstruction, of sentences once sent,
Revisionist ghostwriters, replacing noble intent.
In mandated messaging, selling our ideals and souls,
Involuntary fascism circulates, spinning from both poles.

Such sanitized sentencing, carefully crafted and selected,
Offend all in the end, sterile tongues equally infected.
A call to all, for our free speech to be protected,
Irrespective of class, our foundation was erected.

So much talk enveloping encryption,
So little said with any description.
A world of words for rebel and reactionary,
Adding volumes to a separate dictionary.
Dangerous consequences for imposing political corrections,
For it leaves losers, sowing the seeds of future insurrections.

Permitting a purity of speech, will require two ears,
Listening to others, in best preventing our own fears.
Poles function to freeze the planet in a stable position,
While warmth lives between, where our spirits can glisten.

Photo by Richard F. Moore

Journey of the Falling Sun

Such an early sun setting,
Falling upon mother earth,
Letting go can be so unsettling,
Leaving the womb of our birth.

A journey accompanied with so little talk,
The silent serenity of this solo walk.
A crisp campfire flickers out in the winds,
Forewarning of winter, as daylight rescinds.

A lonely beam glances across western waters.
Gazing over the vastness, a solstice ember falters.
Quiet now spawns some primal reflections,
Easing our fears, healing perceived rejections.

In search of kindred spirits, sparking souls to embrace,
Upon watery reflections, observing my Universal space.
In this place of paradox, and wintry isolation,
I pray all fallen sons will spring to reawaken.

Richard Francis Moore

An Invitation: Without Expectation nor Limitation

In purposeful expression, an attempt to convey,
An invitation for opinions on the future today.
Starting with the creation of a time not to rush,
Periods to brainstorm, where we listen . . . then discuss.

A commencement of only two or three,
Unlocks the isolation of thinking separately.
Releasing one's spirits to further be free.
A modern day model for this new century.

Yet an old thought, an ancient vision,
To speak and share, without derision.
To seek and care, supporting a solution,
Facing life's trials, in renewed resolution.

Outside of family and professional forces,
Unemotional insights, from other resources.
Growth in spirit, career, and also in thought,
Potentially others, will be drawn and sought.

No expectations of some grand new scheme,
Nor limitations envisioning a new theme.
May it live many months, or momentous years,
Ideas in action can overcome any fears.

Wherein our thoughts lead, in time we do see,
Wearing our hearts, is required dress in life's mystery.
One thing is certain in discerning our destiny,
By engaging others, we set ourselves free.

"CHARTING"

Unlimited choices, in traveling life's course,
In limited time, alternatives kind and coarse.

To aid in our outlook, a compass and a clock,
Listening to inner voices, vaulted values we unlock.
Foolish or folly, the good and the great,
Decisions abound, some timely, some late;
Others yield a smile, and a laugh out loud,
While some bring joy; of those we are proud!

Clocks correspond to our schedules to read,
A compass directs the heart, for our life to lead.
Opposed to methodically fulfilling our obligation,
A compass restores reason, routinely adding to creation.
Aiding our view is the clock and compass,
Clarifying values, new pathways do surface.

Unlimited choices in traveling life's course,
Uncertain voices can resound with remorse,
To limited time, with results kind and coarse,
Yet unlimited choices foster a creative force.

Initially imagining our own personal revolution,
Opening options, from the heartland to the ocean.
Fighting our fears, clouded by negative emotion,
The sun shines, blessing both thought and motion.

Altering our course, our chronicle we chart,
Drawn toward destiny, a mystery of the heart.
Many signs are felt, while some we see and hear,
Discovering boundaries, equates to a new sphere.
But boundaries lock and limit, as they first appear,
And freedoms are lost; liberating us to shed a tear.

Illusory limits appear in traveling life's course,
Can provide a correction, and redirection reinforce.

We knew from the start, when we set out to sea,
Not being faint of heart, is sailing life successfully.

51

In such unstable seas, to maintain our vision,
We need be grounded, in our personal mission.

If not yet founded, make it your mission today,
You shall be astounded, on course you will stay.
So in your uncertainty, do not be dismayed,
Time and courage yields your chart displayed.

Everything under Creation (The Sun and the Moon)

Artwork by Jimi Tutko

Seeing through the Darkness

In the closing of our eyes, hear the silence within,
Gaining insight and vision from our place of origin,
Here one may better view the truth in our hearts,
Enabling the stars to guide global fresh starts.

By understanding our place from deeper distances,
Beyond the reach of our immediate circumstances,
By shedding light upon any current curses,
By altering our course, humanity advances.

So embrace everything under God's great creation,
As we can freely choose our mutual salvation,
Available at any moment, for one and every nation.
Just observe the false foundations,
and join anew in our recreation.

Light and Dark

Be wary of all that shines much too brightly,
Watch a magicians hands, move ever so slightly
That which seduces us to the highly visible,
Showcasing the loudest, and most often miserable.

Supporting foundations of false paradigms,
Displaying only what it wants us to view.
A Fractured mirror hides revealing signs,
That could lead us to a peace to see anew.

Fragmented reflections only multiply distortions,
Of further separation, and escalating disproportion.
Misdirected beams of light emit a shattered confusion,
With warlike drumbeats, that deafen our solutions.

Keep a healthy distrust of what you think you see,
As we stage human dramas, in our tragic comedy.
Looking back in your mirror, all may not be as it appears,
History reveals our illusions, with the passing of years.

Reflections for Healing
(Your Optional Journal)

Chapter 2

Early in the Journey
Understanding the Silence

Did any relationships between contrasting aspects of silence and healing catch your attention?

Did you gain any insight or understanding in regard to various contexts of silence this chapter?

Can you identify any silently implied paradigms that serve as a foundation of modern world?

Did any poetic mediation prove insightful or helpful in any way?

Your Other Notes:

Chapter 3

A Cry in the Wilderness

Understanding Change and Chaos

Biographical Briefing

I happily entered my early adulthood, experiencing great joy and much measurable success in both my personal and professional life. By my late thirties and early forties, however, I would be caught off guard as a sustained period of serious life events left me feeling as if everything was coming unraveled all at once! Reminiscent of the adolescent period following my dad's and brother's deaths decades earlier, my perceptions left me with a sense of losing control and confidence, increasingly questioning my abilities and occasionally my very sanity.

Not unlike my adolescence, I began a fresh reconsideration of everything I had once thought or accepted to be true. Call it classic midlife crisis and/or depression, whatever the description, I sensed I was losing my way! At home, my children's own adolescence now challenged my parenting skills with unanticipated frustrations. Other forces of change were simultaneously unfolding in countless ways, beginning with our aging house that no longer served our family of five so well, while my once-vibrant career now seemed suddenly stagnant. Financial concerns loomed larger, and serious family health issues became unrelenting and life threatening for my daughter and my wife, who were each diagnosed with brain tumors. These biblical plagues akin to Job's seemed to descend over me during an intensely difficult decade, ending in 2000 with the suicide of a pastor who was a dear friend of mine and with my mother succumbing to her battle with cancer.

Seemingly besieged by these circumstances, the usual theological and philosophical counsel proved impotent in relieving or reviving my spirit. I watched the promises of conventional wisdom leak from their sievelike foundations, leaving only a shallow pool with which to quench my deeper thirst for healing and renewal. This crisis of collapsing convictions led me into a parched and lifeless landscape that exposed me to recognizing many traditional religious understandings as lacking. I eventually began to view some of organized religions tenants as merely well-intended efforts to provide simplistic answers. Personally, my disillusionment grew as I revisited the often dogmatic decrees I was raised with. Though these age-old theologies were traditionally embraced by pastors and congregations, my heart increasingly felt they were well-intended but nevertheless co-complicit efforts to construct Band-Aid like answers that lacked significant depth, at least for the healing I sought. Overall, I was merely observing how at times we all attempt to fit God into man's more manageable image.

At the same time, my public life paralleled my personal disillusionment and was mirrored in some shared national experiences during this general period where two infamous terrorist events took place domestically. First was the 1995 Oklahoma City bombing, and later was the carnage of 9/11. Both these events demonstrated the almost-universal sentiments of irreconcilable sorrow and inadequate explanations for such unthinkable hatred or justifications for such destruction! Like so many others, I wondered what could the aftermath of such a deadly silence possibly have to say to us all.

No one who knew me was likely to detect the level of my internal despair and increasing stealthy emotional self-isolation. Feeling more alone than I was in reality, I literally began to sink myself to dangerous depths, where I would privately imagine death as some sort of possible resolution. I not only damned the torpedoes, but I also upped the ante to curse damnation itself. If my experience was meant to be some divine form of redemptive salvation, it would have to be revealed to me! Let me explain.

First of all, I believe that honestly sharing our experiences with each other is an important ingredient in healing all of our lives. Of course, I am *not* suggesting we recklessly bare our souls to just anyone, at any time or place. Until such time as humanity is more evolved, I think it is important to be prudent in selecting another trustworthy being to speak with about our most personal experiences regarding your own sacred truth. With this understanding, I have in retrospect consciously chosen to openly share some low points in my life for the expressed purpose of supporting our individual and collective healing. Subsequently, I am ignoring that voice of my ego that says, "Do not risk embarrassment and criticism by sharing the truth of my life." In actuality, I fear no such humiliation, and I am neither proud nor apologetic for sharing what is simply my actual life experience.

With my perceived sense of being alone in a "wilderness," I decided to challenge God and all of creation in the cosmos to find some meaning surrounding all this personal and global suffering. Concluding that my cumulative despair was taking me nowhere, I decided to demand answers from the universe. So it was that one October day, I would impulsively launch my beloved eighteen-foot powerboat and venture out alone onto the open waters of Lake Ontario. With weather conditions unexpectedly deteriorating, I was now about to get what I had not so carefully wished for. Somewhere between the shores of United States and Toronto, Canada, I found my once-placid environment quickly be disturbed as fierce winds and foreboding clouds rapidly approached. In my desperate prayers, I uttered an intention for God to hear my cry once and for all as I earnestly but boldly raised my Job-like fist to biblical skies. Like a bad Hollywood script, the atmosphere cooperated with my melodrama, providing larger waves and rumbles of thunder as bolts of lightning erratically arrived and rains descended upon me.

Continuing to raise my voice to the heavens, I screamed into howling winds for my creator to either show me a way forward from my malaise and melancholy or to just take my life in that moment; for this was his chance now if he wanted it! Blinded with hard rain and covered only by confusion, with reluctant conviction, I dove deep into the rough waters! In my desperation, I had designed a test for the heavens, concluding that if I could ever manage to swim back up and get back into the boat, I would assume it was a sign I was meant to live on, and my answers would eventually be revealed to me. Clouded with my rationalizations of courage and cowardice, I was pathetically prepared to meet my maker and, hopefully, with loving mercy!

Yes, of course, this was jaded, unbalanced, distorted and plain crazy, but it happened, and I chose to share at this time and place for a healing purpose. I obviously do *not* recommend such a course of action for anyone to imitate, anywhere, anytime! God knows we have enough unnecessary pain and drama in our world without needlessly adding to it further as I attempted. Even looking back, it is hard to say how serious I was, for I was good swimmer who dove into those normally life-giving waters, and I immediately thought of my wife and children whom I so loved. Time slowed in such a circumstance, but what seemed like forever may have been only an instant before I decided to swim forcefully back up to try and resume my life as it was.

So in the depths of my downward personal plunge, I chose to give life and my loved ones one more shot if possible. With great effort, I began to swim back up and frightfully struggled to catch up with a boat steadily drifting away with gusty winds and waves. Swimming with all my energy, I managed to eventually take hold of the boat's ladder I had left out (just in case) and eventually climbed back into my boat exhausted. Lying there breathless for some time, I fully grasped that these seas would also prove a very difficult challenge for a small craft to navigate many miles back into the safe protection within the lower Niagara River. God still had his chance to *angrily* take my life if he chose to (as I had been ceaselessly taught about God and his righteous anger with man). With lightning and thunder intensifying, waves began breaking all around me, and I felt real fear. Interestingly, I began to focus on my family, and my determination to live increased as rapidly as my heartbeat. What seemed like hours slowly subsided as I finally made it safely into the protection of the river.

In the following days and months, I would pray (not so much an audible prayer as envisioning my best visions and unspoken heartfelt feelings) that these clouds of chaos would lift to reveal the sun warmly shining upon me, revealing fresh insight and restoring the great joy I had previously possessed. I endeavored to let go of things I had no control over and open myself to new resolutions to old dilemmas. In time, my vocal "cry in the wilderness" would slowly fade as the dawn of a new age in life gradually unfolded before me.

Considering this account of my *wilderness experience,* it is important to examine the nature of change in relation to the connections we all share with the larger dramas in the public arenas of life. It is these episodes that get played out tragically or heroically on our global stages and unfold among the various nations, cultures, religions, and groups that make up the human race. Just as individual traumas can change us, so too can global calamities. Natural or man-made, they can powerfully influence the cultural conditionings and reshape behavioral patterns and paradigms to re-form the future.

For example, was humanity ever really the same after a world war, a global depression, or the first atomic bomb? Similarly, but from a more positive perspective, discovering electricity and penicillin and going to the moon have influenced humanity to change with these awe-inspiring advancements. An exploration of this aspect of our existence could be partially summarized by saying that in regard to normally accepted societal behaviors, *change* usually only occurs after a desperate cry is heard, be it in our world, our own home, or our personal wilderness. The old adage that "the only thing one can depend on in this world is ongoing change" begs us to view the dynamic of change a bit differently. Perhaps we should at last embrace change and even consider rolling out a welcome mat as we progress through our various stages of life?

Changing the Culture's Clothing

Every era, every society, and each generation has them—key beliefs that are understood to be the core values of a given culture. These beliefs, or sacred cows, as they have been called, inevitably give birth to the expression of these values by individuals in all aspects of their life, be it within one's home life, in the workplace, or in the public square. As individuals uphold these values, they are then collectively lived out in all of our institutions, cultures, and nations around our globe. These beliefs produce a set of presumptions that influence how we interact and treat each other daily and how we choose to envision the future, positively or negatively. All the resulting realities that ripple outwardly around the world are born from these cornerstone beliefs, which I have facetiously labeled as *absolutely relative core values.*

Some playful historical examples have included such transitory "absolutes" as

- the sun revolves around our world;
- the earth is flat;
- the ship is unsinkable;
- the sun will never set upon our empire; and
- our nationality is a superior race.
- (For fun write your own examples of former "absolute truths" that are no longer true for society, or for you personally.)_____

Try identifying your own "sacred cows," those *absolute* beliefs you might view as ever unchanging?

For what purpose did we originally embrace them?

Name specific beliefs you were born into, inheriting beliefs by fate or indoctrinations by default (Precepts that you did not personally choose).

What significant core beliefs or understandings dominate our world at this moment in history?

Which values are you in agreement or disagreement with? Why?

Do these perceptions of reality remain because they are forever true, or is it possible that our present values are also in an inevitable transitory state?

To aid clarification, some reflection might be helpful in gaining perspective on chronically changing values. Interestingly, looking back, it is quite probable to discover that many values we embrace as traditional were at one time revolutionary new concepts but over time have been cast into the rigid foundations of the present-day status quo. (The American Revolution is a great exhibit for this picture.) Try and reflect upon how such revolutionary changes in past generations eventually get absorbed into the status quo of society. Once accepted, these new values seldom like their place to ever be disturbed in any culture or group.

Understanding this pattern, the ever-present question remains as to whether these once-innovative values still serve us (or humanity) today. Might history unfold to again expose our once-solid foundations to be deteriorating and increasingly ineffective? Perhaps some previous values were based upon limited knowledge or misunderstandings and, consequently, did not effectively serve humankind, or they were simply another phase of relative truth fading away in light of new discoveries or insights. Minimally, many societal values may just need some shoring up from the universal erosion of time.

Truly positive change often only occurs when individual *free will* decides it is so. If you are content with your life, you may not wish to change anything. If you are satisfied with your membership in organizations, institutions, nations, and world, then you also may not desire any change. Just remember that the collective results of our societies and the greater world are a shared result of our individual and collective consciousness. If we choose to remain unaware of our impact upon the whole, it is ultimately at our own peril (e.g., the extreme example is the apocalyptic image). In short, we all share responsibility for the condition of our world. Conversely, even when we remain passive, change still continues in constant motion all around us. A very insightful treatment of this topic of change is offered in a book written in 2009 by Neale Donald Walsch, titled *When Everything Changes, Change Everything.*

In this context, we clearly have a choice, and one may at least privately opt to courageously question age-old concepts that continually find us repeating our tragic historical patterns of endless war and violence, homelessness, and starvation around our globe. Other questions also beckon us to answer such as

- Having recently been empowered by new technologies that increased our global communication capabilities in unprecedented ways, is this not the perfect time to conduct a universal discussion on what we all truly value, and what we desire for our children and generations to come?
- The escalation of ill-fated and inhumane patterns is now easily and undeniably visible in its global scope. Can we afford to continue ignoring the suffering we can now see?
- How many global calamities result from outdated falsehoods, be it religious, political, or economic?
- Aren't we now aware their time tested catastrophic results threatening the future of all beings on the planet?

- Do we possess the courage to freely choose to examine our most primal values by questioning what was once unquestionable?
- If not, why not?
- Opposite of courage is *fear*—is it what keeps us back from saying what we really want and thus continue creating exactly what we fear?
- Has fear been an effective long-term deterrent in changing behavior? (If so please, prove this.)
  - Has capital punishment stopped more murder?
  - Has "thou shall not kill" ever ceased the declaring of wars, which are so easily justified by governments and so regularly blessed by religious leaders?
  - Beyond the obvious, what is this fear all about?
  - Fear of what, and why, and of whom?
- What values or paradigms are we clinging to that leave so many countries chronically at war, leaving so many citizens without food, water, clothing, shelter, education, or medical care?
- If all we can offer is that this is the way of the world and the way it has always been, is it any wonder we produce a feeling of hopelessness in so much of humanity?

So then, what is the very foundation of our understandings of who we are? What precisely is the fabric of our belief system that now appears as such a tattered garment for our human family? Will we ever decide to weave new clothes that better fit us if we are to have a future that protects us from our murderous history to date? Would you not fit your own children for new clothes as they continually grow in age and size through the many natural developmental stages of their lives? Can we do more to promote growing healthy in age and grace?

We could "fittingly" say that it is time we sew a more universal fabric to protect us from the unnatural disasters of artificial separation, hatred by acknowledging that in a real way, we are all "cut from the same cloth." Just as we were first born in nakedness, it is only natural to consider reaching out to first to heal and cover each other's wounds. Remember at last our original united state of creation and our destiny for divine reunion! Our social, spiritual, and scientific human diversity reminds us that we are cloaked in many colors and that we may again proudly wear that proverbial many-colored dream coat as a divinely styled garb. Together we can design new well-fashioned foundations for a happy future and be more fittingly dressed for success.

Seeking perspective from a more current public story relating to this subject of changing social values and times, let me share an experience I had relating to indigenous native populations. One Thanksgiving eve, I had just returned from a two-week trip out West for the UB nursing school. In meeting with nurses in various Western states (North Dakota, Minnesota, Arizona, New Mexico, Colorado, and Oklahoma), I was exposed to an unanticipated theme. While interviewing nurses in these regions, a number of them specifically reference their work with various Native American populations. They shared their general feelings of heavy lament regarding their direct involvement with the ongoing struggles of indigenous peoples across the North America. While most people are generally aware of the deep wounds of this part of American history, there remains a largely ignored and overdue opportunity to more deeply understand where our prevailing culture can at long last and acknowledge the long suffering of our Native American cultures. More importantly, we might then begin to address our mutual healing.

This circumstance immediately drew me back to a different but equally tragic historical comparison regarding race. Martin Luther King Jr. once spoke of the need for healing, but he surprised his audiences when exhorted black Americans to first to consider forgiveness. Citing his book *The Strength to Love*, he felt that the key to reconciliation, peace, and true freedom with white America would ultimately rely upon black Americans having the courage to forgive those who perpetrated such suffering upon them for centuries.

For Native Americans, the need for acknowledgement and reconciliation remain first and foremost in order for any meaningful process of forgiveness to ever potentially present itself. With respect to any premature talk of forgiveness, there needs to first be a fundamental recognition and societal understanding of the depth and magnitude of injury that has so tragically occurred and undoubtedly remains silently resonating in the psyche and soul of the surviving remnants of America's indigenous populations. It is timely to restate this book's purpose here, remembering that we are *not* writing to focus on blame but are seeking balanced perspectives for the understanding and healing of all.

With a vast majority of U.S. citizens being descendants of immigrants who often fled their own persecutions from many cultures, we in America need to reach out in heartfelt authenticity to begin a truer reconciliation of that which is ultimately irreconcilable. Only then can we finally begin to know each other and begin anew and benefit from the wisdom native Indian cultures have to give us and our world. As the original caretakers of this land, one might rightly suspect that they still have the keys to many secrets of this continent for our mutual healing benefit and our common future together.

One similarity to our more recent recognition of the historical ills of slavery, our pledge of "liberty and justice for all" always challenges us to face each other with genuine efforts to understand of our shared experiences, whether happy or sad. When we act upon this, we will strengthen the future, bonding a foundation built upon a relationship of mutual respect between peoples.

As the first section of this book remains centered on both the *past* and our Declaration of Independence, it seems appropriate that the intended spirit of thanksgiving needs to at last be recreated in balance and genuine harmony with each other. With equal footing, we can rightly celebrate the bounty of Mother Earth's harvest as a blessing with our diverse nationalities also being gifts to share together. This must someday come to pass in a more real way, beyond our romanticized and imagined historical reconstructions. When it does, it will serve to bless all of us with a new beginning! Such is my prayer that prompted me to pen this Thanksgiving poem.

Photo by Richard F. More

Thanksgiving: An American Original
(Amoriginal* Lament)

Fleeing persecution and deprivation overseas,
Immigrant ancestors desperately and courageously boarded ships.
Leaving behind family, bringing ancestral tales,
Despite fearing the unknown they set so many sails.
A foreign and intimidating landscape they described,
Trust was cautiously sown between settlers and tribes,
Despite the distrust of help with lifesaving provisions,
Feeding immigrant bodies despite suspicious divisions.

Some accounts speak of two cultures helping each other,
The common language of spirit, innately helps a brother!
Such cultural sharing always holds great potential to learn,
As witnessed by the combined creativity of European confluences,
Sharing together with innovation, created a new world of influences.
Yet the unintended sharing of disease, costs many lives and cultures,
Fueling death and conflict, fears would rise by feeding of vultures.

The accounts of Thanksgivings origins, so many tales now old,
Stories we are proud to portray, perhaps inaccurately told.
Regardless of the many versions, and conflicting truth,
All versions likely capture important fragments of the past.
Aboriginal peoples became our country's outcasts!
Demonized as savages, setting the stage for justifying persecutions,
With ironic cruelty, immigrants flee tyranny, to begin executions.
Eventually escalating a genocide blessed under Christianity.
Thanksgiving must first acknowledge this past insanity.
Until together we sit down at the same table,
Respectfully embracing in thanks to the creator,
For plentifully sharing our gifts of each other,
Communicating as Americans, as sister and brother.

If we are to ever reach the heights of our expressed ideals,
We must finally own our misdeeds, broken treaties and deals.
Such recognition is a key to everyone's healing,
Our reach can open a door for our pardoning,
To restore hope for all by reconciling,
America needs forgiveness for a healthy renewing.

This visionary hope is within America's sight,
To those who hungered, huddled in fright,
We can now embrace, and no longer fight,
We have the courage, and use real insight!

Then we may freely give true thanks,
For the native families of this land,
Who had cared so well for Mother Earth,
Preserving this continent with sacredness,
With a spirituality that speaks to the intent of Thanksgiving.
On bended knee we pray to heal one gentle step at a time,
Healing wounded knees and all sides and injuries,
So much unnecessary separation and deprivation,
Let us begin to know each other, beyond reservations.

How can we deliver freedom to this whole nation,
A deliverance from Native American lamentations.
Let us return to a real celebratory horn of plenty,
Asking Americas natives to forgive our original sin,
Of trying to destroy God's gift of the American Indian.

Let Thanksgiving be renewed with its best intention
Holding up a cornucopia of loving potential,
Honoring the rich cultures of our Amoriginals,
In the best traditions of an American original,
Thank God we can at last be free harvest our bounty!

*Yes, I am suggesting a new term intended to show respect and honor the original inhabitants of the North American continent and indeed the western hemisphere as America's "Amoriginal" peoples.

This is but one example of change that has the potential to free ourselves to speak more honestly in civil tones with each other and can help us unlock the boundaries into which we sometimes box ourselves into. How else can we rise above the current lack of public discourse that continues to drown out real listening and sink us all into deep trouble by intentionally polarizing the public! With a good-natured smile, President Ronald Reagan used to joke by saying "that liberals had gone so far to the political left that they had left the country." In today's debate, it could humorously be reversed to suggest that the political right has gone right out of their minds with self-righteousness that they are also bordering on leaving the country, exiting stage right, if you will.

Like President Reagan, it can be funny, but in reality, such characterizations are destructive as they only serve to vilify fellow citizens and ignite additional arguments that have no winners. We all lose when two ears are closed and singular voices grow ever louder yet remain unheard. It is as if they had never even spoken a word in the first place. I have called it decibel deafness, and in this atmosphere of chaotic clanging, hearing is not possible! This dynamic is quite the opposite of our previous reflections on silence.

A thought regarding this current state of public discourse so marked by chronic posturing, spinning, and polarizing poses some questions.

- What does anyone not get about the futility of extremes?
- For example, would you paddle a canoe on one side only?

Of course not, for you would end up going in circles, literally going nowhere at all or maybe becoming stranded on the left or right shore. We will all need to use both paddles in navigating life's changes. It is my belief that we cannot continue to grow on the journey of life if we are no longer flowing naturally in relationship to all. So again, without judgment, let us at least begin by listening first and then take pause to thoughtfully consider other viewpoints before expressing just how we genuinely feel. Preferably, we can do this without automatically replying with the expected "correct" answers or only repeating those socially acceptable values we are all conditioned to speak within our particular upbringing and social groupings.

Our cultural values are often summarized by political leaders as the "fabric of our society," but over time, outdated values can wear thin, often becoming a torn and tattered fabric. In time, even societies need a change in cultural clothing, not so much because there was anything inherently wrong with those appearances but because we have grown as people. Let us grow in age and grace as we each pause to privately reconsider our own values in relation to each other. After all, we are related to each other.

In this light then, how do you truly feel about present day conditions that continue to produce unacceptable acts of inhumanity that continue to be justified by so many sides? The world eagerly awaits your own answer.

"So let us not talk falsely now, the hour's getting late" (Bob Dylan, "All along the Watchtower").

The truth is it is getting very late.

Concluding this chapter titled "A Cry in the Wilderness," we reflected upon moments of both great societal and individual despair, examined the anguish of fractured communities, and observed the natural human empathy displayed during national and international calamities. Thus, the poems ending this chapter reflect the rawest expressions of our heartfelt prayers and utterances from deep within ourselves. They echo our confused cries of conflict with one another with wails that endeavor to reach the ears of governments and or God. These verses invite us to again seek the blessings that come with an increasingly enlightened civilization! These exhortations are sent out to reverberate in our ears and simultaneously resonate in the hearts and minds of men and women everywhere.

I continue with reflections on these themes beginning with a poem that looks back upon my fortieth birthday in a condensed retrospect during decade of periodic trauma. In the end, my wilderness experience helped my rebirth and my personal transformation with a heightened awareness as being an equally strong and vulnerable member of the human family. Beyond the wilderness, we all must forge on upon our life journey.

Come Forth from the Wilderness

For forty days and forty nights,
A wilderness fraught with frights,

A fasting of feelings over forty years,
Firmly fastening so many fears,
Dreams drowning, capsizing careers,
Illusions dissolving, vision disappears.

My sinking spirits I could not dissuade,
As topical depressions unleashed a stormy decade.
Ironically, idealism's collapse reduced my tomorrow,
Decadence would not have produced such sorrow!

So dark a night, a sleepless sleeping,
No sign of light, I yielded to weeping.
An eve so prolonged, still lying awake,
I longed for some movement, for God's sake.

Discord created friction, a disease of our vision,
Degrees of dysfunction, a dying sense of mission.
Such sparse energy, yields paralysis aplenty,
A lavished futility, over analysis of insanity.

Richard Francis Moore

A cry in the wilderness, a search for some sanity,
Just demands of heaven, in my cursing so saintly.
Imploring a holy answer, without the complexity,
Finally tasting some truth, I digested the simplicity.

Emerging from this darkness, breathing so still,
Focusing only upon my own will,
Distantly glimpsing a glimmer of peace,
Cooling my fears, flaming fires did cease.

Aflame with new energy abounding about me,
Incinerating constraints of any perceived scarcity.
My senses renewed, as I returned to caring
In abundance I remembered an original sharing.

Answers then came, solutions would show,
Only a few at first, and then more could flow.
Forgoing the past, and suspicions of ego,
Trusting my intuitions, forward I did go.

Reacquaintance with community, via forgiving,
Resecuring sustenance, a renewed way of living.
Revealing a new dawn, for my new age,
Reviving love, removes the residue of rage.

Seceding from past decades and fears,
Watering renews growth over the years,
Utilizing tears that were annually cried,
Flowering anew, my joy was multiplied.

Forty cycles expanded my circles of friends,
Ever expanding a universe that never ends.
I embrace each moment as never before,
Eternally loving, I am encircled forevermore.

Forward to a Future? Or a Void?

Improving the world, spinning in circles all around!
It will be conquered, a destiny secured and found!
The quality of life will be mastered and measured!
No longer in doubt, secure whatever you treasured!

A new millennium for man's metals to be tested,
A thousand more years, can peace to be wrested?
The quality of life, we will master and measure!
Without fear or guilt, we pursue any pleasure!

In the age where man and iron are cast as machine,
I hear scraping and screeching sounds eerily careen.
Honoring the harsh and horrid, the crass and crude,
Dishonoring of the old, by the brash and the rude.

Such scary sounds, can prove cruelly cold,
Searing the souls, of both the young and old.
Children's formative faces, eye monitors with a glaze,
Monitors scream their views, upon violence they gaze.

Times are fast and furious, suppressing the glorious,
Histories are lost, subduing the mystical and miraculous.
Comics copy cynics, sadly achieving the hilarious,
As humorous self-indulgence is taken so serious.

Four seasons now merged into one frenetic pace,
For undefined reasons, quickly moves a human race.
Racing somewhere to win; but what and why for?
In losing our solitude, heart and spirit seem poor.

Schools mix with pharmacies, compounding minds,
Earth's revolutions continue, with a force that binds.
The quality of life we now measure and master!
Achieving even more, granted wishes grow faster!

Who would wish a return to the centuries of old?
Millenniums of massacres, buries a death so cold.
We are now at the threshold of a future so bold,
Men as masters, mastering man in ways untold.

Betterment of our bodies, increasing longevity,
Confused in our hearts, with feelings of brevity.
Science the sacred cow, slays legend and lore,
On Technology's altar, altering human rapport.

The millennium's magic, we hurriedly package,
Will it replay the tragic, of our historical wreckage?
Coming so far, conquering problems in progression,
Does a full moon rising, lead full circle to regression?

Trusting Innovations to make us physically whole?
Must solutions sacrifice a searching of the soul?
May a balance be found, if we give it fresh thought?
A sensing from our souls, within our will it is sought!

Improving the world, opportunities comes around,
Is the answer in forgiveness, freeing love to abound?
For love leaves a legacy, displaying a peace that is seen,
Replacing a void, releasing remnants harmful and mean.

The sun rises again for our futures fresh chances,
Will we use it to celebrate, as humankind to advances?
If we master our world, what will be our new measure?
Has human history foretold, what is truly our treasure?

Speeding forward to a future, still positively annoyed,
Leading toward our true destiny, or a place to avoid?

Ism's

Polarities succumb to many schisms,
Two wrongs equal self-righteous decisions,
Multiplying crusades, or righteous fanaticism,
Or leaning to the left, we kill a czar for Marxism.

After defeating tyranny in the form of fascism,
The void is then filled by dangerous militarism.
Lies are manufactured under McCarthyism,
Justifications to brand innocents with Communism.

Is it self-interest on a scale of national vandalism,
Or are they freedom fighters decorated for heroism?
Perhaps an ethnic cause, or some new nationalism,
As the same old atrocities, ignore all rational criticism.

Making more waves, flowing from a tide fundamentalism,
Dating back to old politics and the swords of Roman Catholicism.
Reformations born again from Protestantism and Puritanism,
Alongside Islam and Buddhism, Hinduism and Judaism.

As religious zealots preach political evangelism,
Theocracies condemn any helpers of humanism,
It is abundantly clear in our world of pluralism,
We must coexist at last, each accepting some criticism.

One Man on an Island

Treading time, one man on an island
Around swift waters not often seen inland,
isolated by this Island's grand moat,
Like spirits reach out, as by they float.

And while these shores, waters surround
I feel their love, and I hear their sound.
Refreshed by viewing, freeing my thought,
I renew my middle aged Camelot.

In the night I turn, then I toss,
Quelling fears of love and loss,
I dream of loving ideally,
Of what is not yet meant to be.
From this isle's point of view I spot,
Looking back upon my youthful Camelot.

Reminded by the water, as it quietly flows,
Reflecting spirits, seeing silent souls.
Still basking in love, long after the glow,
I remain united to all, each being I know.

Separated by this Island's grand moat,
Like spirits reach out, as by they float.
And while the shores, waters surround
I feel their love, hearing their silent sound.

Surrounded by water, though safely on land,
No longer dreading time, one man on an island.
Water under the bridge, cleanses my thoughts,
I renewed my love in a new age of Camelot.

Defying Deaths Darkness

I
Darkness dominating,
Daring deities to strike me dead,
Detach me from all that is dark
Definitely disengage, disembark!
Dehumanization does deploy,
Demeaning life, we continually destroy.
Damaging delusions, damning us to death,
Designing Illusions, denying us fresh breath,
Destructively divisive, dogmatic derisions,
Detouring deliverance, with diabolical divisions.
Displaced and misplaced doctrines,
Defaced documents deliberately doctored,
Deceiving designs, institutionally polluted,
Drawn up to be, decisively diluted.
Destroying visual signs, decidedly desensitizing,
De-Facto blinding, and brutally binding,
Deafening and dumb, defeated we succumb.
Depressed senses further repressed,
Dialect disappears, under the thumb.
Discretion declines, desecration is nearing,
Differing degrees of increased fearing.
Deception thrives, as dissension deprives,
Deeper descending invariably arrives,
Delivering distance and darkening our days,
Disturbances distress us in finding our way.

II
Declaring devotion to a deity,
Daring defend our duality,
Deceitful deliverance disguised instruction,
Defending deceit, demanding destruction.
Decrees of scripture, encrypted with delusion,
Delay the truth, with degenerative illusions.
Depreciation and deprecation, despite pleas
Defecation covering earth's nations,
Depleting resources, dispensing rationalizations,
Describing deities who'd destroy their own creations?
Delusional wars, defend deadly doctrines,
Delaying the disappearance of a damned illusion,
Decay and decimation in the name of sin,
Disguising salvation, denies us redemptive dawning.
Dear deities, dry your eyes,
Drop your hands from imposed deafness,
Dumbing and numbing common sense,
Deliverance from death we now dispense.
Declaring our loving destiny, can end the pain,
Defying this design, of death's illusory reign.

III
Dressed up in dollars, disguised dignitaries,
Dangle deceitful doctrines,
Delivering deplorable indignities,
Designed to detract from our divinity.
Deliberately Dante-like, an infernal design,
Dominating humanity's debilitating decline.
Doubling divisions, of each generation,
Dismembered we are by such separation,
Duplicating our dual degradation.
Disappearing oneness, both human and divine.
Denigrating what is wholly sublime,
Unholy decrees are diabolically defined.
Demeaning all who dare display insurrection
A death defying act of resurrection.
Deeply sensing our dysfunctional deprivation,
Deliverance drowns in such times,
Defeat predetermined, we decried,
Dialogue destroyed, definitively denied.

IV
Discovering truth under deep layers of dirt,
Discarded details do not dismiss the hurt.
Deliverance forever follows a different drummer instead,
Disregarding our dilemma, no one gets out of here dead,
Distilling ourselves from our well-aged souls,
Delighted spirits dance
Determined to proceed from disquieting conditions
Deepening love, delivers our contrition's.
Driven to the surface, describing our elation,
Decreasing by degrees, our perceived separation.

V

Departing our cocoons, we now free ourselves,
Determined we destroy, deaths damning notion,
Damaging Ds now disappear in synchronized motion.
Behind this rainstorm, the sun of God always shines,
Dawning and delivering abundant times
Delightful blessings, radiate after rain

Dreamed of paradise, our perfect terrain,
Deeded as our original state of being,
Redeemed, we reclaim upon seeing.
Destined for this creative living landscape,
Daily death tolls we dare to escape.
Deliverance born out of the goddesses,
Degeneration ceases, rebirthing creation.
Embracing love, all pain deceased,
Decidedly sunny, dethroning disabling dictates,
Defying death's darkness and illusory reign!

Chapter 3 ends with a global appeal in response to the horror we witnessed on 9/11, with impassioned cries from around the planet for greater understanding and support of each other.

For many days after the infamous carnage of 9/11, I wondered why the world's religious leaders were not all publicly holding hands together while making bold new pronouncements in faithful unison that we are all God's children, all in one family, identically created in love! Such compelling questions continue to demand answers especially from religions leaders along with governments and all our institutions. For God's sake, and for everyone's sake, we pray religion soon lives up to its purpose and potential in professing and exemplifying the love of God for all creation.

What Have We Sown?

I was birthed and then baptized,
A submerging of salvation, did man capsize?
Why are some disdained as wholly unsanitized?
Who ordained others unholy and marginalized?

Assured that your soul is certainly saved,
Recruiting more members in this spirited phrase?
As judge and jury render infidels depraved,
Executing edicts, ordering orthodox ways.

Bow to Allah, for yes, God is great,
The Quran covers this good news.
Yet should death be ones faithful fate,
If not fully conforming to rigid views?

Reflecting upon Buddha's pure quest,
That millions still quietly pursue,

Meditations purity positively suggests,
Godly conflicts cannot possibly be true.

Intentions for the Hindu,
Seem similarly true,
Living for liberation to truly pursue,
Discovering bliss is already within you.

If a people are specially "chosen,"
What stones will then befall me?
Shall not thou be in damnation,
Without heaven or safe haven to flee?

Be it the Bible, or any faith further evolving,
A book of Mormon, or reformations revolving.
Do new inspirations separate present from past?
Or do golden plates create new divisions to cast?

Right or wrong, Is one chosen or not,
Is a soul either saved, or condemned to rot?
Heated debate, judging the good and bad,
Fostering hatred, renders our religions as sad.

God's own children, he redeems or condemns?
Religious intermediaries intervene with amends?
Is denominational dominance righteously rewarded?
Are competing theologies then mutually thwarted?

Every faith seems fractured in two,
Catholic or Protestant, pray tell what is true?
Islamic conflicts between Sunni and Shiite,
Intersecting violence over whose sect is right.

Wherein lays all these heavenly proofs?
What is really being spoken under religions roofs?
Is theology in alignment with an all-loving creator?
Or is it broke and betrayed by the fruits of its labor?

If proof is measured in actual outcomes,
Has religions recruitments, yielded any lessons,

Richard Francis Moore

What have the centuries witness accordingly?
Remembering to "forgive seven times seventy"?

I do not believe Buddha, Jesus, Mohammed or a Dalai Lama,
Nor a god or goddess, decreed this hateful human drama.

Faith preaches that were to love each other,
One human family, as sister and brother.
Purportedly created in God's loving image,
Men create a devil to blame for their carnage?

Do you approve of humans spiritual history?
Unholy paths are no longer such a mystery!
Disciples so faithful to kill and to maim,
As apostles secured a most worldly shame.

What is truly being sown with all of this preaching?
Has religion been faithful, and true to their teachings?
So you be the judge, for the divine is within you,
Will we reach out in love, or preach hate to continue?

Speaking to your creator directly,
No need of holy men or hierarchy,
Seeking your peace from the heart,
For within you is love, you are free to impart.

So let your spirit lead your body,
By your actions God is known,
By simply loving everybody,
The seeds of salvation are sown.

Reflections for Healing
(Your Optional Journal)

Chapter 3
A Cry in the Wilderness
Understanding Change and Chaos

Did you note any relationships between the nature of change, chaos, and healing and growth?

Did you gain any new insight or understanding(s) in regard to various aspects of change?

Can you identify any shifting paradigms that may be resisting or reshaping our modern world?

Did any poetic mediation prove insightful or helpful in any way?

Your Other Notes:

Chapter 4

A Ray of Light

Understanding beyond Oneself

Sharing makes prosperity more shining and lessens adversity.
—Cicero

Photo by Richard F. Moore

It is universally understood that new growth upon earth is fostered by rays of sunlight. When combined with fresh air, water, and fertile soil, the growth can be beautiful and bountiful, but even under these optimum conditions, time is required for germination.

Continuing with the book's first act emphasizing the past tense, picture closing your eyes to imagine rewinding our life memories by reviewing our personal path of Independence to date. Our replay is a purposeful attempt to consciously shed light upon our own chronological growth. As our ongoing maturation process continues, we might benefit by observing life through this intentional retrospective lens. Here one might better appreciate whether or not past recollections or beliefs have served our life well and whether they continue to be helpful or detrimental as we move forward in life. An uncomplicated example is to consider if some of your adolescent beliefs or young adult convictions remain relevant or truthful at this time. Can you recall and identify your personal beliefs earlier in life? Did they serve to productively benefit you, and if so, have they changed over time? If some of your beliefs have changed, how have they? If not, do you ever pause to question these earlier precepts as possibly only partially true and effective? Simply put, do those older beliefs provide the positive solutions and outcomes you had hoped for as you have grown older? With open eyes and an open mind, take some time to look past our inherited youthful beliefs to see if new light can be shed your life as it has uniquely unfolded for you. In my instance, this exercise feels like an ancient revisiting of my childhood and adolescent years.

One of my favorite recordings during my teen years was a vinyl album by the Rolling Stones titled *Through the Past Darkly*. In retrospect, the album's unique octagon-shaped cover held some coincidental symbolism as its stop-sign shape could have warned me that looking backward too frequently may not be a good way to view life. If we find this a habit, perhaps it is a pattern we might consider stopping. Nevertheless, our intention here is a positive effort to seek insight on our life.

Citing my experience was a familiar reference for many 1960s adolescents, and this brand of rock-and-roll music resonated deeply within my own chaotic experience. Beyond some of my personally challenging circumstances that I have already shared, suffice to say that this historic period (1960s) was a dark time for many, and not just those experiencing normal teenage confusion. I have come to believe there is much truth that teenage conflicts are born out of the fact that adolescents often see with uncomplicated clarity the insanity of the adult world they are about to enter. Left with choices that seem hollow to them, they continue questioning the state of civilization as they know it because they observe the manner in which adults have acclimated themselves to a world they see as broken but their elders accept as normal.

The 1960s was marked by both a hopeful idealism and instability as social transformations also unleashed a fearful resistance to change. Significant paradigm shifts occurred at breakneck speed as is well documented. Massive peaceful demonstrations were held while others turned violent as citizens rioted over issues ranging from the military draft, the war in Vietnam, civil rights regarding racial division, along with many fundamental freedoms long denied to women. The results often left entire sections of many American cities literally burned to ashes and under martial law. I would personally witness these unfortunate scenes in Buffalo and Niagara Falls, New York, as well as in Detroit, Michigan. These conditions were in fact sustained national occurrences during this decade, leaving much of the American population emotionally inflamed, impassioned, and fearful from coast to coast. Adding to this public chaos were the well-documented assassinations at all ends of the political spectrum—first with President Kennedy and later his brother Senator Robert Kennedy, Dr. King, Malcolm X, Megdar Evers, and the attempted assassination of Alabama governor and presidential candidate George C. Wallace.

I was not alone in my feelings that the national psyche was left wounded, arguably with a void of national leadership and an unquestionably polarized population now piling up an emotional garbage heap of cynical public distrust. Such an atmosphere fostered an escalating political paranoia on all sides and slowly contributed to a poisonous atmosphere that would eventually even consume the next White House in the Watergate scandal that concluded in the resignation of President Nixon. One could make a case that the level of antagonistic gridlock in the U.S. federal government (early in the twenty-first century) remains a byproduct of this era. Again we are reminded different opinions can serve as a source of democratic strength when we listen to one another, but when it crosses the line into mutual vilification, the tone deafness results in polarization and political paralysis.

While this lack of trusted leadership was felt by many citizens around the world, for me, it was even more personally pronounced with the tragically corresponding death of my father. As my widowed mother was left behind (at age 49) to fend for her nine children, life became personally threatening far beyond the prevailing political insecurity. Stunned and devastated, our entire family entered the saddest of personal storms, each member carrying their own legitimate story, perspective, and life challenges. Like others in similar circumstances, I instantly assumed many adult responsibilities that left me anxious and fearful. In spite of my innate playful nature, the levity of my youth was overcome with an unavoidable heaviness where I privately gave way to many tears. The weight of these burdens would linger on for many years, just as it would uniquely affect each sibling who ranged in age from 7 to 23.

Now as I look through that past darkness so many light-years later, I can finally see how these tears baptized me into my adult life at age 17. In hindsight, one can argue that they served to cleanse me and released within a nourishment for much personal growth. My tears eventually combined with fresh air and the sun's warm rays to germinate new growth slowly blossoming in and all around me. It was only in retrospect that I would come to see how my painful youthful pruning eventually flowered into the joy I desired, after long eluding me during repetitious cycles that only produced habitual sadness.

Within this radically intense period of my adolescence, it often felt as if I were helplessly cascading downhill along with the flow of my tears to somewhere unknown. Despite the uncertainty, I actually wished I could just drift away from those sad circumstances. In my daily anxiety over negotiating these deep currents, I was slowly opening up to welcome any changes to my circumstances. While desiring to just release it all, I remained a contradiction as I was intermittingly reluctant to embrace the very changes

I sought. Occasionally, I would go to yet another extreme by jumping beyond the present and senselessly worry about the future. As we grow into adulthood, such big leaps can naturally lead to stumbling, which I did. As I repeated this futile pattern of inconsistent action followed by a paralysis of worrying, I eventually was able to look back and happily discover I had actually made progress along the way in terms of growth and maturing. In hindsight, we come to know that most people relate to this tendency, helping to provide us with a clearer picture of life—that picture being that we are never completely alone in this shared human experience despite our unique personal circumstances.

Like others, I would revisit this pattern of past, present, and future concerns at seemingly supersonic speeds as if I were fueling my own internal cosmic time travel. This erratic yet rhythmic ebb and flow could behave as one powerful tide controlling my personal seasons. This recirculation of the same old stormy cycles tired me, but with maturing and conscious decision making, I eventually found relief through occasional breaks in these clouded conditions. Like any dark weather patterns, bright beams eventually break through the clouds and uplifted my sight and hopes to view the shining light above. With these moments came an increasing ability to balance the emotional extremes that accompanied tensions over the past, my sobering present realities, and the future.

Some years later, in a quiet moment, I noticed a particularly beautiful ray of light shooting through a modest opening in the distant sky. I was struck by the fact that it was made highly visible due to the existence of the surrounding darkness of an exceptionally black and cloudy night that was hiding a full moon. This singular moment felt as if it may have been provided for my unique personal observation, only to be seen from where I stood, while understanding, of course, that the full moon exists for all of us even when invisible to the eye. Similarly, the following two occurrences help shed light for me on the many ways we all share so much in common together and thus potentially offer us lessons in our mutual need for our individual healing and caring for one another. Recalling these experiences of adolescence and early adulthood, the lessons I absorbed would ultimately help me navigate the many stages of life yet to follow. Here are but two instances that helped demonstrate this healing potential.

1. Applying the previous observation to my personal midlife plight (perhaps a moonless midnight plight would be the better description) where I was struggling with the daily challenges of raising three teenage children. Here I experienced a moment when I "had seen the light." It was during these naturally challenging

moments of parenting my own adolescents that it finally dawned upon me that I had a simple choice to make. Being the adult, the simple choice was either to just love my children unconditionally or to require certain conditions in order for them to receive my love and acceptance as a reward for their compliance. I gradually concluded that such an inflexibly stern stance may garner their temporary but superficial compliance, only to someday result in inevitable failure. Such a tactic might have sown the seeds of muted resentment or mutually repressed anger over the doubts of self-worth from feeling only conditionally loved. My children had unknowingly provided me the opportunity to grow even deeper in *understanding* love, a more perfect form of love, less religious but godlier, less righteous but more spiritual, less emotional but more heartfelt, and more personal yet increasingly global in its implications.

2. In my professional life, I had recently left a twenty-year career in the YMCA movement and was now working in an executive fund-raising capacity for a school of nursing at a large public university. My duties included individually surveying nursing alumni across the nation as part of a strategic planning process. During the time of this employment, there was a five-year period where my wife was stricken and treated for cancer. I am happy to write that she has survived and recovered wonderfully after undergoing distinctly separate cancers involving innumerable modalities, protocols, and treatments.

During this traumatic time, nurses unexpectedly supported me and taught me more about healing than I could ever have imagined. Aside from their usual practical advice, I was hearing so many surprisingly positive reports about holistic and alternative therapies to complement the existing protocols of Western medicine and their accompanying technological advancements. Their insights shed new light for me on healing, with fresh perspectives for current treatments and a balm for old wounds, be they physical or otherwise. These nursing interviews awakened within me an inquisitive curiosity, to be followed later by a greater understanding of our internal power to heal ourselves and thereby begin restoring our own natural and healthy state of being.

This was the end of one road and the beginning of a process guiding me away from the past, releasing me, and freeing me to pursue ever new pathways on my life journey. Beyond my personal circumstances, it was during this time that I became even more deeply committed in my professional mission to garner increased philanthropic support for the causes of nursing and healing in general! After all, I had now very personally benefited from nurses as they reached out to serve me and my family in many deep and positive ways—ways that were unexpected and transcended my limited understanding of healing.

Beaming *(Photo by Richard F. Moore)*

Biographical Briefing

Our never-ending growth and development opportunities contain an innate desire to discover our destiny or simply seek answers to the question of who we were born to be. As a youngster, I recall being very inquisitive and preoccupied about ultimate questions of where we come from, who made us, etc. I am certain I exhausted my mother with unceasing follow-up questions to the answers and information that innately feels incomplete to all of us. This verbal pattern of mine continued throughout my grade school years, although it was not always appreciated by the good nuns educating me. Despite my rote memorization of the dogmatic Catholic catechism and corresponding good grades in religion, my spiritual questions only multiplied.

My teen years would reveal that I was reading comparatively peculiar material in contrast to my peers and siblings. For example, I read Mahatma Gandhi's autobiographical *Experiments with Truth*, followed by every book ever written by Martin Luther King Jr (*The Strength to Love* was my favorite) and Erich Fromm and *The Prophet* by Kahlil Gibran. I went on to read many different Bible translations and volumes on comparative religion. This led me to read the Quran, the Bhagavad-Gita, Book of Mormon, texts on Buddha, and the *Tao Te Ching*. Swept up in the idealism with which the 1960s initially began, my youthful questions soon became a passionate quest to discover *truth*, a pursuit I would carry into my college years and beyond

I mention this to draw a connection to my midlife quest to renew this focus, only this time with much more life experience to draw upon. As I assessed new views beyond the constraints of orthodox structures, I began reading texts outside the narrow limits of religious traditions with many new authors (Neale Donald Walsch, Deepak Chopra, Marianne Williamson, and Eckhart Tolle were a few). In addressing spiritual themes, they utilized many refreshing views while not discarding the potential for religions to at last fulfill their professed loving purpose. These new perspectives did however help demonstrate religious and denominational biases and their accompanying efforts at conversion that often fostered competition and conflict. In observing differing religions, denominations, and sects condemn each other, it is historically documented how many efforts were made to righteously prove other theologies and faiths were somehow flawed, if not totally blasphemous to the "true God." Such efforts all risk creating more separation, fear, hatred, and violence, rarely producing the unity of a loving God.

Much of my effort to achieve new understandings were fueled by what I increasingly viewed as a world that remained tragically trapped in repetitive cycles of destruction. Resisting any utopian naivety, I sought practical and realistic counsel. Now more concerned in my children and future generations, I decided to actively seek out the expert advice from the words of living leaders in a various disciplines beyond the narrow scope of religion and spirituality. Beyond my earnestness, I also tried not to take myself too seriously. For instance, I would intentionally try to lighten up by smiling and thinking how the late comedian Rodney Dangerfield might humorously respond to all this soul searching. In his self-deprecating demeanor, he might be apt to say, "Hey, what do I know? I may as well go ask the crazy leaders of our world just why they lead us into all this #@%^*@#!" To me, it is a funny image with which to ask the big questions and not at all inappropriate, for who else should we begin asking but those holding power . . . or ourselves? If those in power are maintaining the status quo, why do we give them power over our lives? With such simple questions, I sought answers from leaders.

Because of where I was employed (the State University of New York at Buffalo), I took full advantage of hearing the many distinguished speakers who addressed the university community in person. On some occasions, I had the rare privilege to meet face-to-face with leaders such as former President George H. W. Bush (photos below) and Colin Powell. Here part of my professional work included attending such functions where our leading philanthropists had the opportunity to meet with these esteemed speakers beforehand.

Credits to Nancy J. Parisi, Photographer

Credits to Nancy J. Parisi, Photographer

Other leading speakers that I was privileged to listen and learn from in person included

Madeline Albright	John Glenn	Janet Reno
Maya Angelou	Al Gore	Salman Rushdie
Kofi Annan	Rev. Billy Graham	Tim Russert
Tony Blair	Alan Greenspan	Carl Sagan
Wolf Blitzer	H. H. The Dalai Lama	Arnold Schwarzenegger
Julian Bond	H. H. Pope John Paul II	Kevin Spacey
Ken Burns	Jay Leno	George Stephanopolous
Bill Clinton	Steven Levitt	Donald Trump
Hillary Clinton	Bill Maher	Elie Wiesel
Stephen Colbert	Michael Moore	Jeffery Wigand
Bill Cosby	Bill Moyers	Bob Woodward
Anderson Cooper	Joyce Carol Oates	Steve Wozniak
Rudy Giuliani	Conan O'Brien	

The timing of each speaker proved exceptionally relevant as I continued witnessing our world struggle to preserve a fragile and questionable status quo. I observed my own country seeming to slip from its once prominent position of leadership in many ways, ranging from manufacturing, and economics, but more importantly, losing some sense of at least seeking some moral high ground. As the world shrinks, global questions grow daily. One example would include questioning the powerful impact multinational corporations are exerting over people and nations. Are they positively developing the poorer countries of the world or merely exploiting them? Are they fostering new sources of green energy or holding them back for profits while further stressing the environment? These issues are complex but critical to address for everyone as it becomes clearer that alongside our independence, we are increasingly interdependent on all nations working closer together.

While I do not profess to have an easy answer to the complex global issues facing our current times, the truth is that each of us ultimately carries an individual responsibility to address them. It is increasingly clear that citizens in most countries are currently gravitating in two fundamental directions.

1. A small percentage are gaining great wealth beyond their wildest imaginings.
2. A majority of citizens are slowly slipping out of the former middle class with many spiraling ever downward into a new more hopeless poverty, out of sight from what was once a mainstream or middle class population.

Such deteriorating conditions support the growth of negatives ranging from homelessness, to ignorance, terrorism, refugees, and more. These results will not logically prosper any economy or country, so those in power must quickly recognize they must no longer ignore the obvious ills. Many other issues challenge our modern lives and times, but suffice to say my focus in listening to these leaders speak was to try and gain insights that might shed some light in empowering all of us to heal individually and then collectively.

These powerful people ultimately reminded me that citizen awareness and personal responsibility have historically proven to prevail as the greater power. The challenge remains, can we—*the people*—do something positive with the information we possess? Historically, it does not seem to matter if the leadership comes in the form of a pharaoh, emperor, king, czar, dictator, president, pontiff, or CEO. In the end, it seems that whoever holds a disproportionate share of wealth and power becomes increasingly accountable to the people they govern over time. This remains true even if those in power fail to understand this fact of life as accountability and responsibility invariably rises to the surface and explodes in some form of reformation or revolution.

Despite the many sobering circumstances of our life in the early twenty-first century, I was mostly inspired by the lives and very personal stories of these prominent speakers along with the many new authors I was now reading. The meditative poems that follow provide a medley of hopeful and transformational themes in the face of very intimidating personal and public problems. Looking back upon my life to date I can see times when I consciously broke from past beliefs and indoctrinations that no longer held truth for me, or failed to positively contribute to fulfilling a sense of higher purpose. Much gratitude is also due to so many unknown but equally insightful individuals whose wisdom helped provide me timely encouragement and guidance over the years. Their loving assistance has shined many rays of light upon the path of my life journey.

"We are not human beings having a spiritual experience. We are spiritual beings having a human experience" (Teilhard de Chardin).

Meditation Medley

Dawning

Eyelids awaken,

Slightly at first, then ever so brightly,
    to greet that day,
        and the infinite possibilities,
            with the potential to unfold,
                if only we notice to greet them in our rising.
All is possible, as my lips and mouth join in an awesome chorus
synchronizing with my eyes,
        Surprising me to form a face now fully smiling,
     centered with my midlife renaissance, in the midst
       of greeting as a new day is dawning!

Breathing
I breathe in deeper than is possible,
in wonderment of the impossible,
inhaling an infinite energy, full of life,
inspired happiness, our eternal essence,
internally residing within,
Simply by breathing it all in!

Nesting
I enjoy our metamorphosis, daily, moment by moment,
welcoming your next sharing of you,
so that I may read and reread you,
coming to slowly meld into your mind body and spirit,
and feeling you slipping softly into me in similar ways.
Flying this morning with more of you, spreading, enveloping,
Never more to be a solo unknown . . .
. . . *evermore* to be uniquely in unison,
more of oneness liberates us from a self-imposed isolation,
bringing sweet nourishment, exposed in our nest this morning.

Diving

With the same boundless blue of the sky and waters,
You blew a breath of life into me and I return my inspirations as well.
Welling up from the depths within us it becomes easy to see friendships
infinite possibilities,
Just as the sun is seen reflecting upon the blue seas, fed from our wellspring
of love, within.

Resting

Good night, good morning, goodwill, and Godspeed,
may your spirit travel, this day, this night
this moment, an eternally good day, every day
Secure in love, resting in joy, resting in all that is good!

Resounding

Earth tones abound, both audible and visual,
Spending time to freely enjoy life's song.
Colorful overtones are eternal gifts.
Attuned to a loving resonance!

With increasing frequency,
Hear the heavenly vibrations,
Diverse melodies echo over the nations,
Through ears and eyes, our mind resounds,
Joining body and spirits, to be beautifully bound.

Body, spirit, you and me, sharing love, singing soul fully!

A Glimpse into the World of Right and Wrong
Do we dare risk to reveal ourselves,
No fear of exposing our rough edges?
As we all possess shattered parts, after falling from life's ledges.
Seeing only right angles,
Fingering blame in a pointless direction,
Righteousness only further entangles,
with our egos fear of rejection.
So many angles can wrongly lead us astray,
As sharp minds and tongues can cut both ways.

Yet our broken parts can also sharpen us,
Cutting through shallow pretenses of life,
Utilizing our disjointed parts to sparkle anew,
Rebuilt into mosaic mirrors we are free to renew,
Upon reflection we cut through our pain and our pride,
Tasting equality, we groom gifts for our divine feminine bride.
Celebrating the diversity of our combined truth,
We inevitably encircle all viewpoints,
Coming around to a place where we can all freely sing our hearts true song,
Overcoming faulted arguments of who broke the mirror of right and wrong.

A brief background for this next poem:

The inspiration of this poem came from my own parenting attempts to convey to three teenage daughters that our culture's pressure to idealize some mythical female physical form of beauty is a harmful message. In addition, I listened to several psychiatric nurses who had expressed their frustration with treating the increasing incidences of anorexia and bulimia—conditions often related to the failure to accept the natural beauty of our own bodies and, more specifically, appreciating our individual uniqueness as our gift to the world. Billions of people, and no two are the same.

Crystal Clear (Photo by Richard F. Moore)

Crystallization
Like each frozen crystal, or fallen snowflake,
No two beings ever the same!
Neither woman's breast, nor male lingam is replicated;
No two bodies alike, nobody twice repeated.
Even twins fail to fully mirror the other,
In exposing the illusion of ideal size,
Concepts of right or wrong shed their guise!

Heavenly bodies, all uniquely positioned,
Over the whole universe, in holy juxtaposition.
In this atmosphere clouds billow by,
With ever renewing shapes in the sky,
Each earthly breath, births a new form!
It is no wonder why conformity is so uncomfortable,
Be comforted in your uniqueness in every way, shape, and norm.

For nothing is normal,
We are all extraordinary,
Every star shines as one of a kind,
Outshining semantics, describes the divine.
A miracle in each moment,
As we discover our own unique design.

Uncovering this truth, upon each crystal we gaze,
Recovering our sight, our spirits are raised.
Healing the fractures from illusions that blind,
Focusing with crystal clarity were pleased to find,
Stardust is common, within each other's eyes,
Our future of loving union is clearly visualized.

Artwork by Jimi Tutko

Echoes of the Heart
Flowing from this chamber,
An observation of the heart,
Serving love over anger,
A resuscitation of loves lost art.

From this heart, read more of me,
Receiving a warmth that love imparts.
As echo-cardiograms help us to see,
Clearing clots, to lighten heavy hearts.

Wounds of anger, or hatred worse,
Blocks loves flow, casting a curse,
Illness is linked to a failure to forgive,
In attacking the heart, we cannot live.

So silently I am sutured,
Touched in the silent night,
My being is again nurtured,
By the hearts intuitive insight.

Abstaining from any cultural judging,
Gently beseeching, never shoving,
Circulating love beyond begrudging,
Acceptance is healing and ever loving.

Seeing the sight of a black raven,
Disrupts the suns warmth upon your safe haven,
As it crosses this luminous beam of light,
Notice that illusory shadows, always flee in flight.

Flowing from this chamber,
From the beatings of a heart,
Echoing love over anger,
The essence of love's fine art.

Sparkling Tears
Banished feelings, barriers for fears,
Finally flowing, freeing pent up tears.
Emotions outpouring, sad all the while.
Motions enduring, until receiving a smile.

Such inner torment, storing torrential rains,
The eye of the storm, lashes personal hurricanes.
Resisting to let go, despite this force that so drains,
Our internal wasteland, we must release the remains!
Spewing forth your sadness, let it all go,
unleash it all, relinquishing from long ago!
You can procure fresh water, pouring it to flow,

refreshing smiles to flourish, and the present to grow.
Tears trickle down cheek, rolling off the back bad will goes,
A cleansing for the body, mind spirit, and souls.
A stillness reveals sunshine, sparkling for miles,

Facing tomorrow, replacing sorrows for smiles.

ALREADY

After the current kiss,
Thoughts of a new day.
As tomorrow we miss,
Our love of yesterday!

Fearful currents will relentlessly sweep,
Emotional foundations to our dismay,
Torrents of tears freely fall as we weep,
While the life we knew flows far away.

The current kiss,
What's next? We say,
Tomorrow we'll miss,
What we had yesterday!

Living no longer, a life devoid,
Remnants leave a hollow void.

We are left stunned and still.
Realities rape our own will.

The current kiss,
Our hearts do pray,
Appreciate the bliss,
That we have this day.

Too numbed for anger,
Left so lonely and lost,
What emotions do linger,
Are feelings frigid in frost?

The present day kiss,
One must now display.
Or the mind will miss,
The memory of this day.

The surviving soul left fearfully alone,
Expression limited to merely a moan.
Other souls now expressly do the giving,
Helping return a survivor to a land of the living.

Not one of us today, could really be ready,
To accept and to say, it is tomorrow already.
Proceeding with life, I now embrace each kiss,
Not regretting tomorrow, I claim my present bliss!

Resilient Seasons

We are all entitled, to our personal seasons,
Some roads are required, to experience for reasons.
Reasons unknown, as things come and go,
Yet surely you have grown, looking back you will know.

So fear not the future, self-centering is not bad,
your balance will be truer, and immeasurably glad!
Such are our seasons, of both darkness and light,
they include many pleasings, unseen at first sight.

****

Loving Atmosphere

Fear not, inhaling fresh air
Meditate, dropping despair,
Taking stock, you have your life,
Enjoy all, dismissing the strife.

Billowing clouds do blow on by,
Darkness recedes to an open sky.
Returning colors to our blinded eyes,
Visions of the wise, old illusions vaporize.

Filling our lungs with renewed energy,
Hearts pump fresh joy, flowing freely.
Facing life's fears, with winds so gusty.
Exhaling the old, that is stale and musty,

Love covers us all, always abounding,
Despite change, constantly astounding.
Stilling your soul, new answers release,
Willing to grow, your spirit finds peace.

The waters again rise, as do the earth's gases,
Tides come and go, just as a problem passes.
Illusions give way to refreshing solutions,
Rain showers nurture renewed resolutions.

Such divine ebb and flow, permit us to grow,
Experiencing life, both the high and low.
Observing many forms of earthly energy,
Embracing our oneness, and spiritual synergy.

Reflections for Healing
(Your Optional Journal)

Chapter 4
A Ray of Light
Understanding beyond Oneself

Have you ever had fresh light shed new thoughts or open up new beliefs to you over the years?

Have your adult years provided you with any new understanding(s) or viewpoints in regard to new societal changes, or in your own personal life?

Societally?

Personally?

Can you identify any paradigms that if reshaped, might positively help our modern world?

Did any poetic mediation(s) prove insightful or helpful to you in any way?
(e.g., "Crystallization"; with nearly seven billion unique humans on planet earth and not two with identical beliefs, how can we begin to more effectively move forward together?)

Your Other Notes:

Chapter 5

A Confluence of Nurses and Healers

Understanding Pathways to Healing

Chapter 5 concludes the first section of this book in relating to our past experiences around the theme of our independence. By further contrasting the realities of our private and public lives, we can seek to better understand the duality of our interrelationship in supporting each other while also maintaining a healthy independence.

Appropriately, this chapter focuses more directly on our subject of healing by examining the rapidly changing paradigms in the healing arts. Focusing upon nurses and other health practitioners, we observe that their mission is essentially one of healing past wounds. While acknowledging the positive impact of all healers upon our world, I draw special attention to the broader mission of nurses including the education of patients and families in preparation to consciously live a healthier lifestyle of wellness and prevention in each present moment.

My professional work in surveying nurses nationally over a fifteen-year period also yielded many personal revelations to me about healing. As a group, they slowly heightened my awareness of the potential benefits for healing from many different holistic, alternative, and complementary therapies. Nurses did not present these alternatives as competing with modern medicine but viewed them as an important complement to existing protocols. Their ideas were often rooted in age-old traditional insights or ancient therapies that ranged from breath work, herbal remedies, and meditative practices like yoga and sometimes explored our psychic senses. Whether using common sense remedies or some emerging new therapies that science has yet to fully study, it is safe to say that these other healing modalities will continue to experience increased exploration by people around the globe. Given the problem that health care coverage has increasingly become too expensive and/or unavailable to greater numbers of people, these therapies may grow even more rapidly as the only affordable alternative for many individuals and their families. For many people on the planet, such alternatives may become the only ones they can realistically access.

While there is no single-minded consensus from the nursing profession on the subject of alternative practices, my sampling would indicate there is a general conviction from many nurses testifying to the benefits of at least exploring alternative therapies on a case-by-case basis. The concept of complementing the beneficial advancements of surgical, technological, and pharmaceutical treatments is not so much one of debate but more a matter of common sense in evaluating other available healing methodologies for a patient's potential benefit. In this light, I did not find any contentious atmosphere that discounted scientific progress but only an openness to researching other emerging effective treatments.

Many nurses summarized their own stories and experiences as having personally received helpful benefits from incorporating more holistic treatments. These included both old and new alternatives alongside the most modern scientific protocols of Western medicine. I might better characterize this topic by sharing a perspective that nurses are helping lead the way to view wellness as the best way of preventing illness. Continuing to work beyond treating symptoms and illness after the fact, they are increasingly focused on taking preventive actions directed at clarifying the many interrelated root causes of illness. Suffice to say, nurses' insightful observations (of patients and their families) continually inspired and motivated me to professionally advance funding for their healing cause.

At a personal level, I was equally interested in seeking nurses' practical advice, including their assistance in directing me toward many alternative health practitioners that I eventually sought out for my own healing. In this process, I have come to appreciate the incredible level of nursing care that has been evolving ever since Florence Nightingale founded the modern nursing profession. In expansive new ways, nurses are providing increased leadership in numerous health care venues worldwide. The wisdom and insight they openly shared with me assisted my growth and healing in immeasurable ways, and the same could be said for my entire family! I owe a debt of gratitude to the many nurses that I have benefited from in a myriad of ways, some of which are included below.

1. Personal Experiences
   - How nurses guided me and my daughters during my wife's five-year battle with dual cancers, which included several invasive surgeries, radiation, and chemotherapy cycles.
   - How nurses helped my wife and me during various surgeries on all three children, the most serious of which was the surgical removal of for a brain tumor on my then nine-year-old daughter, and followed by eye surgeries
   - My own heart attack and follow-up surgery. From the ER to the recovery room, nurses provided so much important information and assistance to fully complement the talented and life-saving surgical team!

In addition to my own related experiences, I now share a few other compelling life stories as told by nurses themselves. I hope this will help your appreciation of the unseen and unspoken healing content that often exists within their daily actions of direct assistance to us as patients and our families.

2. Nurses Sharing Their Own Stories
   - Shirley DeVoe, a nurse I had the privilege of meeting with many times over a decade, had sadly passed away shortly after I had left my position at the university. At one point, she had shared with me the sobering start of her life as a nurse. Shortly after her graduation to become a nurse, Shirley bore the grief of receiving the news that her fiancé was killed in the attack at Pearl Harbor. Not long after that fateful day, she enlisted and found some solace in utilizing her nursing skills by serving the troops in the Pacific Islands during WWII. Speaking about just some of her heart-wrenching experiences, I was touched by one in particular. During those rare pauses of high alert and an often overwhelming number of critically injured patients, the USO tried to boost morale with socials and dances. She noted with so few women present, she consciously tried to dance all evening with as many soldiers as possible. One night, she believed to have danced with over one hundred servicemen! Despite finding a sense of meaning and some satisfaction that she had brought some smiles to many lonely men, it did not lessen her deep pain from the loss of her fiancé. After the war, Shirley worked as a nurse for the VA throughout her career and remained active in the reserves. I came to know her as

an exemplary philanthropist for nursing causes and as a warm and caring person. While Shirley never chose to marry, not surprisingly she did build a noticeable network of close relationships over a lifetime. I was fortunate to have known this generous and loving person.

- The late Margaret Nelson was a decorated nurse who served throughout WWII in the European campaign, including the infamous Battle of the Bulge. She described her situation as so dire as to require her to perform life-or-death surgeries due to there not being enough doctors to ever treat the numbers of wounded soldiers. With no other choice, she and other nurses served as surgeons by default. One can only imagine the mental, emotional, and physical stress and more! After performing surgeries, Margaret did not rest but would often spend her remaining daylight hours taking bandages off the dead and washing them out as best she could in a nearby stream. Knowing they were out of clean medical supplies, she prepared for the next day as both nurse and surgeon!
Margaret passed away in 2010, but she left behind many legacies, not the least of which was an endowed lectureship fund to her nursing alma mater that will provide an annual lecture for students to hear from a leader in the nursing field. What a gift to future generations of nursing students and faculty!

- Requesting anonymity, another Vietnam-era nurse chose not to convey the details of her war experiences but did choose to share that "I witnessed things that no human being should ever see or experience." This reticence indirectly spoke to the eventual recognition of posttraumatic stress disorders (PTSD), which is now well documented but was not so understood at the time. This is yet another example of the unspoken power of a nurse in action as this nurse went on to professionally help support others afflicted with PTSD.

Of course, military service is not the predominate venue in which our society benefits from the incredible range of care from nurses. Our society is daily touched by caring nurses in hospitals, clinics, a multitude of community sites, and in visitations to many homes. The aforementioned individuals returned to civilian nursing in various capacities ranging from veterans hospitals, school districts, psychiatric settings, and higher education to name but a few. They graciously and thoughtfully shared their personal stories for strategic planning purposes for their alma mater, in relation to our asking them to respond to the nature of healing at all levels. To me, their raw firsthand reports and dramatic stories provide insights for our healing and recovery in ways that transcend mere words. I hope these accounts might also serve you with a heartfelt appreciation of the nursing profession and in relation to your own healing processes over time.

A few summary observations about healing that came out of my individual interviews with nurses follow.

Not unlike any social group—be it ethnic, religious, political, or professional—there was no singular point of view on what nurses expressed regarding the most important aspects of *healing*. Nevertheless, in reflecting upon my nearly two decades of involvement, the following theme did become clear to me as one overriding collective message was to view our health in overall terms. One nurse spontaneously expressed it by viewing health as a wheel with many spokes connecting to the center of a healthy person. She avoided saying holistic due to stereotypical images and any semantics that might detract from her point, which was to remain open to each spoke as being a single unique treatment that may have some potential healing benefit in the future. She quickly added that we also resist being enamored by a favorite therapy by embracing only one or a few healing modalities, be it an accepted modern practice or some ancient traditional protocol outside of science per se. Her point was that all treatments may have a part to play during one's lifetime, even if just for one moment. It might be that one could benefit from an unorthodox alternative which could assist with a special healing solution. Perhaps the perfect complement to your prescribed treatments at just the right time and place.

Using her imagery of spokes in the wheel, envision being in the center of the wheel, where the attached spokes connect us with many healers revolving around us. While each connected spoke may conceivably need repair over time, we can easily see that the cycle of life invites us to explore the entire world around us. To get more metaphoric mileage from this mental picture, we tread on, as ultimately we are in fact at the center of our own health management. We are obviously responsible for steering those tires onto the paths in which we are led. Upon our journey, we can draw strength from exercising as these spokes support us by preventing wobbly wheels, and thus avoid any unnecessary bumps in the road. Yet bumps will occur, and repairs to our health are part of the physical world. Putting the brakes on this cyclical imagery, I offer the following poetic expressions of appreciation and encouragement to the nursing profession and the many other gifted healers helping restore the health of our world.

Wikipedia, Wheel Of Life. (bhavacakra from Bhutan).

In the Spirit of Nursing

So full of spirit,
Loving by listening,
To unknown patients,
Generous in giving,
Peace via patience.
Sensitive soul
A solace so softly appeals,
As Your hands touch heals,
An eyes glance emancipates,
Receptively you reciprocate.

In silence, the soul you touch,
Firmly affirming, healing much,
Silently sutured,
A being is nurtured,
Healing so wholly,
Holistically healing.
A nurse is such a welcome sight,
Serving both by day and night,
Penetrating the darkness with light,
Intuitive gifts offer heartfelt insight.

Skillful soul, soulful spirit,
Loving by listening,
To patients unknown,
Gracious in giving,
Peace is patiently sow

Richard Francis Moore

Nursing's Mission

Where to start, who's to say or know,
Saving lives, CPR for the heart and soul.
Treating illness with many interventions,
A segue into the world of preventions.
Beyond present protocols are new inventions,
Delving deeper into healing intentions.

From resuscitations and intubations.
To managing a patient's pain cessation,
Internally resulting in soothing sensations,
Eternally touched beyond documentation.

Management of all this and so much of that,
Beyond comprehension and job descriptions,
Be it surgical or pharmacological prescriptions,
It results in treating innumerable afflictions.

Applying new technology and medication,
With each renewing breath is life's restoration,
Even overwhelming odds, knows death is not failing,
As all outcomes yield an emotional exhaling.

Adding intuition into the medicinal fix,
A nurses ingredients blend a therapeutic mix.
Not only intuitive, nursing is also creative,
Increasingly this quality is substantiated,
Being both quantified and more qualitative.

Fusing science and soul, an inevitable linking,
Combining logic and love with critical thinking.
In spreading salves, inside hospital doors,
Or sewing open wounds, closing topical sores,
Treating outside, and under the skins surface,
Beyond any limiting boundaries they face.

Humanity hurts outside a clinic doors,
Beyond the spaces within hospitals floors.
Adding to the treatment of many an illness,

Elevating discussions into the heights of wellness.
Nurses rise above any present occasion,
By grounding families with a healthy education.
Who can capture this mystical mission,
For the practical scope of its caring vision,
Is simply too comprehensive to document,
To voice any singular uniform statement.

Merciful Nightingale

In a culture deprived of much feeling,
Thank you for tender touch,
The teaching of touch,
Healing touch.

A balm for the body broken,
Words need not ever be spoken,
Our good senses simply hear it,
A salve for the injured human spirit.

A nurse knows of pains root causes,
Bared and exposed in life's silent pauses,
Nurses also assist in our spirits enduring,
By touching feelings, a disease begins curing.

Songs so sweet from this nightingale,
Soothing such a discordant human wail.
From Florence wings spread to caringly avail,
Restoring our strength, that may again set sail.

A soothing psychic union,
A medicinal holy communion.
Treating wounded souls sensibly,
Stitching body and spirit imperceptibly.

Healing with touch is so essential,
For spirit, mind, and bodies so sensual,
Nurse, Goddess, and God are mystically blended,
As health is restored and miraculously mended.

Richard Francis Moore

"I think one's feelings waste themselves in words, they ought all to be distilled into actions and into actions which bring results" (Florence Nightingale).

Nurse-speak Unspoken

A growing awareness of metaphysical forces,
Of auras, and chakras, and unseen resources,
From psychic, to tantric, and energy fields,
A knowing sense to use these protective shields.

While not yet quantified by physical science,
With qualified research by bona fide scientists.
Yet humanity climbs toward knowledge's tallest peak,
Science scales the west side, metaphysicians the east.

Up through low-lying clouds, and then past the tree line,
Into the cool crisp air, revelations from the sunshine.
Where science and spirituality ultimately converge,
At a point where creation and big bangs merge.

Approving all life, upon our planets paradox,
Proving we are all one, and our universe rocks!
Be it the third rock or another distant galaxy,
The energy of life, enlightens our living mystery.

No need for sides struggling, of right or left,
Categorically right or wrong, leaves all bereft.
Journeying up life's mountain, be calm and content,
Knowing at the top, will be mutual enlightenment.

So what is a nurse, what of her speech,
As her silent actions inaudibly reach,
Healing thru many modalities, curing much,
Born of science and spirit, a healing touch!

So nurses have taught me about their practice in essence,
Perhaps best expressed by their unspoken healing presence.

In closing this chapter, the final poem (Holistic Highway) addresses the many alternative therapies I eventually sought out and utilized for a variety personal health reasons, in addition to other resources such as some very beneficial pet therapy for our family ranging from dogs to rabbits. I elected to write a humorous treatment of the subject, but be assured I was seriously helped by many of these modalities, often to my own surprise and amazement. A quick for instance was related to my chronic back problem (located at the fifth lumbar/first sacral) bearing ever-increasing sciatic pain over forty years from a congenital spina bifida. I had repeatedly tried all the usual protocols, from exercise, diet, physical therapy, spinal injections, medications, podiatrists, orthotics, chiropractic, and reflexology

My search ultimately led me to see Maya Yonika, a shamanic healer in Ashland, Oregon, who had experience in the use and flow of Kundalini energy or energetic healing. She described our session as a "rebirthing ritual" that might help begin healing my pain. I was informed that various stages of this treatment combined the therapeutic use of disciplined breathing techniques and energetic touching and that during this treatment, I might experience the feeling of my extremities numbing, in addition to the likelihood that my memory might vividly replay much of my life before my eyes. I was asked to not be concerned about this but to have faith and just follow her directions on how to rhythmically breathe at varying prescribed cadences, and I would be fine. We then practiced them, and she assured me that her voice and touch would guide me through a helpful healing process. She inquired if I wanted to proceed, as she needed my faith and heartfelt cooperation in order for us to make this an effective treatment. I expressed my comfort and free will desire to proceed.

We then began, and as I followed her instructive breathing techniques, I fell into a very relaxed state of being. I was fully conscious of her voice, but I was also sensing a surreal experience, with time slowing and as if I were just witnessing it all from above. As cautioned, I began sensing my limbs going numb. She spoke reassuring words to me that all was proceeding fine and that next I would likely begin to witness many memories flashing back before me, and they might trigger emotions as vivid memories can do. It was periodically emotional as I began recalling some specific moments of my life from early childhood up to the present. In addition, I clearly remember one other strong sensation—that of very warm energy traveling inside the length of my spine. It felt as if warm water was flowing through a hose attached to my spinal cord gently running back and forth from bottom to top and back again. At this point, I felt so alive yet strangely in a state of deep peace! It was as if I were outside of my body, peering down as a calm observer. She continued speaking to me with a gentle guidance as we slowly returned to breathing more normally and quietly as she ceased speaking. As my arms and legs regained their feeling, I returned to a more regular state of relaxation and consciousness.

What thought was about an hour-long session shockingly ended up being an astounding two-to-three-hour treatment. I felt like I had awoken from a slumber though I remembered all that had transpired and felt relaxed yet very alert and happy, but more significantly I was feeling no pain.

I had many questions about the amazing and mystical quality of this experience, but as I began to inquire, I recall her just raising one finger to her lips with a gentle *shh*, explaining that I should rest now, but we would talk again later. We did visit later that day, where I began asking my *logical* questions. After patiently listening to me, she answered with genuine humility and in very few words; she merely reminded me that many traditions and cultures have historically used healing touch, not the least of which were Jesus and many who followed, reminding me that Christ had tried to tell people if we only had faith the size of the mustard seed, we too could touch people's lives with amazing healing. She said the most important lesson I should take from this was that I do not need her—or anyone else, for that matter. She added that each of us is a child of god/goddess and thus possess a divine capability of healing divinely implanted within us from the beginning of time. The problem she expressed is that we have temporarily forgotten who we truly are.

Later on that day, I was still not satisfied with such general answers, and I pressed her with more questions, seeking greater understanding of what had transpired in our healing session especially after I began realizing that I was no longer feeling any back pain. She smiled and patiently tried to convey the following (and I am no doubt paraphrasing her clumsily).

The mistake of science, or faith-based belief systems, is that both leaders and their followers fall into the complicit trap of so desiring to explain everything in simple and quantifiable terms that they attempt to establish dogmatic definitions for an infinite number of individual divine responses to each of us. So it is impossible to define unique healing treatments in definitive terms as every unique person is unlikely to have identical experiences. In fact, she added that acts of healing are akin to lovemaking (never truly twice the same), requiring the faithful and earnest participation of two beings (giving and receiving as almost indiscernible) for a true fulfillment of the hearts creation and the body's healing. With that explanation, my time to leave had arrived. She then gently hugged me to go in peace and love for all, with the reminder to meditate daily and do my prescribed yoga stretches and breathing exercises in order to aid my continued overall healing.

More significant is that I went the next eighteen months without one moment of back pain! In that time, I did not take one medication (not even a Motrin or Tylenol) and never iced down. Previously, both of these practices were done many times each day, year in and year out. While a recent MRI still shows the existence of my birth defect, and I have occasionally needed medical support, the long-term change for the better has been unprecedented and astounding. As I write this chapter I am now in my midsixties, and for nearly ten years, I have been over 90 percent pain free, which has not been true since I was in my teens. Wow!

I openly share this powerfully true story with no need to convince anyone of anything, since there is nothing I have to sell. No newsletter, no membership, nor any religion to join. I can only leave you with the awesome sense that somehow we are all divinely human and directly connected to an intelligent and miraculous source. Many times I am just in awe as I recall nurses first helping to expand my awareness to better *understanding pathways to healing* as they first spoke to me about their observations about "healing touch" and its many meanings over the centuries and in this modern world.

Changes in healing continue to shift at incredible pace just in my own lifetime, let alone a century ago when women's health and female physicians were virtually nonexistent. Since beginning to write this book, unimagined new approaches such as the utilization of medical marijuana, and cancer vaccines, robotic nanosurgery are only a few visible examples of emerging new paradigms in healing.

Now for that more lighthearted poem I promised regarding my odyssey of pursuing holistic therapies.

Holistic Highway

I asked nurses for some candid advice,
About deeper healing, it needn't be nice!
It need not be refined, or politically correct,
I only cared about the healing effect!
Tell me where I might seek other answers,
For me and so many wounded bystanders.

So they told me their truth to go here and there,
Dropping past notions, and breath in some fresh air.
They told me I'd discover new methods of care,
Some may match my needs, if only I'd dare.

So I began with chiropractic,
For some relief of my sciatic.
With all my nerve, I took action into reflexology,
One foot at a time, they treated my whole body!

Richard Francis Moore

Seeing my way forward to an iridologist,
Was I becoming a serial seeker of therapists?
Back to a more socially acceptable visit, to an LMT,
Then a Reiki master followed with some herbal tea.

Later drawn to a psychic, as if magnetically.
In balance I pursued polarity therapy,
Next was a shaman that treated me,
A curious calming, almost sub-consciously.

Before you knew it, I took another progression,
To my Akashic reading, and a past life regression.
Then I stepped back with some sound nutrition,
Then an herbalist, adding ingredient additions.

Taking a time out, for I was moving too fast,
I slowed the pace, by enrolling in yoga class.
But my congenital sciatica, continued to flare,
So I turned to acupuncture, yet a new form of care.

I planned a spiritual retreat, a healthy cessation,
Only for reading, organic eating, and meditation.
Yet there would be more, as I tuned into Tantra,
Learning ancient practices, and many a new mantra.

Making time for astrology, and exploring my birth sign,
My Gemini twin tried to make sense of my design.
A more tame experience with an aroma therapist,
Breathing in healing scents which were hard to resist.

From feng shui for both my office and home,
To all of these healers, I never felt alone.
Next came Chinese medicine, but I avoided colonics,
My not trying everything seemed funny and ironic.

Magnetic items clung to my clothes for a while,
But they did not always fit the occasion in style.
Many a diet, I would be open to try it,
My family would laugh, saying I was a riot.

110

Yet spiritual readings, combined with power,
I was energized, both daily and by the hour.
Then energetic healers, and rituals of rebirthing,
Their breath work astounded me, a new unearthing.

Add kinesiology, and some crystal therapy,
How could I be less than fully happy?
As the spokes of the wheel had spoken to me,
I felt better by the year, bodily and spiritually.

Taking time for my health, I now better help others,
From family and friends, loving all as sisters and brothers.
In healthy retreats, I to minister to myself,
Lovingly we manifest, wellness and health.

Reflections for Healing
(Your Optional Journal)

Chapter 5
A Confluence of Nurses and Healers
Understanding Pathways to Healing

Have you ever tried new approaches to healing that you once viewed skeptically or even as nonsense?

Have your adult years provided you with any new understanding (positive or negative) in regard to conventional or alternative health care in society, or in your own personal life?

Can you identify any paradigms that, if reshaped, might positively help heal ourselves or our world?

Did any poetic mediation(s) prove insightful or helpful to you in any way?

Your Other Notes:

ACT II: THE PRESENT MOMENT

A Declaration of Interdependence

(Chapters 6 to 9)

Whether or not we consciously choose to leave the past behind in its ever frozen place in history, our reality in this present moment will unfold regardless as to whether or not we are paying attention. Our reality is as they say, *a gift of the present moment*, and it is ours to fully experience and live if we so chose. If we fail to open up this *present gift*, is of course, our free will choice. It is worth differentiating between learning beneficial lessons from past experience as opposed to remaining fixated on the past and risk stagnating ourselves in a sleepwalk-like state of dysfunction.

Within the very presence of each microsecond awaits a potential world of wonderment for us, if we but knowingly approach it with our spontaneous spirit of unbounded creativity. By approaching each subsequent present moment in a similar state of awareness, miracles can begin . . . in the next unfolding moment of . . . *now!*

Come with me and let's test drive the present . . .
That was then . . .
. . . Now I present yet a new moment here . . .
. . . There it went . . .
. . . Here is another one now . . . whew . . . wow! *Fast!* Now is now and not the time to look too far ahead or bother looking into the rearview mirror (as things may appear closer than they really ever are) since we blew past that scene so long ago. Watch out as another moment has arrived to live in and just enjoy *"being in"*!

Enjoy every single miraculous moment in its endless new unfolding. Whoosh! Each heartbeat, every fresh breath of life, and every new opportunity is meant to be whatever it is and whatever you make it be! You were born to live in this time and space! This place and in this moment is your destiny for today, and one really can't think too much about it. Instead we need to relax into the flow of spontaneity and just be in the here and now to smile, laugh, hug, kiss, cry, and experience what you feel now.

Simplistic, perhaps, but the profound truth is that your joy *depends* upon allowing your inner power to freely and fully experience each moment in the world at large. More than that, it will help you create glorious next moments. Yes, even in those moments that don't feel good, such as those negative and agonizing times like the loss of a loved one. One must first understand that difficult times can also lead us to a healthy pruning and into new personal growth. Growth, however, *depends* upon choosing to positively cultivate our lives if we are to harvest the happiness we desire.

Let us consider this word *depend* and how it relates to our present situation here in the twenty-first century in a world where we are increasingly interdependent upon each other—from electronic communications, education, the production of goods and services, growing infrastructures for transportation, financial transactions, environmental concerns, and issues of sustainability that all of humankind is challenged with at this moment. It is apparent that our modern-day interrelationships are growing as a healthy interdependence that can increasingly be mutually beneficial for humanity at this time. As you observe so many fast-paced changes for yourself, you no doubt notice how some old paradigms, social mores, and laws are often quite different from those in earlier decades. The popular adage that "change is the only constant we can all depend upon" is and has always been accurate. Our world is ever changing and will so remain. No need to list examples as you can easily identify innumerable changes for yourself. The purpose of the second section of the book is to invite the reader to embrace participating in helping create positive change in the present moment as opposed to fearing the unknown future moments. Change always includes new opportunities for both pruning, new creation, and growth, but fearing change freezes us, and if left to fester, it can sow seeds of destruction. As always, our free will presents us with a choice to shape those moments of change now.

This interdependence is not a condition up for debate, approval, or rejection, for it simply reflects our intensifying present circumstances of change and may even shed some new light upon our often debated human-divine natures. Our natural state of being has arguably been one of humanity moving ever forward to reconnection, communication, and reunion despite appearances to the contrary in our chaotic human history. At times, it might seem to occur at a glacial pace, and at other times, it might seem too fast and frenzied to grasp. Nevertheless, history does keep moving on. So it is time to recognize the reality that no man or woman ever was an island, and we find ourselves to be increasingly interdependent upon each other for so many aspects of our daily life. This dynamic will only escalate for our children and grandchildren. With conjecture, I explore this topic as having the potential to be seized as a happy and merciful evolving toward the restoration of our original state of being, which was to be together in the first place.

Prepare yourself then to notice and be mindful of the joys and blessings before us, and then consider embracing these times with your fellow beings as we stand to benefit by reconnecting and relying upon each other in new and beneficial ways. Fear not change, for this represents an opportunity for a Declaration of Interdependence naturally flowering before your eyes during our present times! This represents a new progression even beyond the understandings of our cherished and visionary Declaration of Independence which has undeniably benefited humankind in recent centuries. In Act II of this book on our healing journey, let us consider creating a healthy interdependence, not by replacing our independence but by actually nurturing ourselves as we grow into a more mature and healthier independence! Now about that joy I referred to.

Enjoying Today, and > the Next, > and Next > . . .

All I need say is summed up in just one phrase,
Upon future foreboding, one should not gaze,
As life in the present, we should enjoy today.

> *Into future futility, let not our minds stray,*
> *Lest emotional volatility embezzles your day.*
> *So enjoy what we have know you are blessed,*
> *Sufficient is the day, and in this we can rest.*

> > *Be unconcerned; don't attempt to overplan,*
> > *As life's uncertainties, we cannot understand.*
> > *In the proper time our needs will be met,*
> > *Fear not the future, nor the past to regret.*

> > > *Can you control your future, with all your drive?*
> > > *Experience says no, no matter how we strive.*
> > > *Family, friends, work, and home are all heaven sent,*
> > > *To be in this day, is to love life as it is in the moment.*

> > > > *So be open to this present day gift,*
> > > > *For human hearts to all uplift,*
> > > > *One singular thought I thus convey,*
> > > > *Enjoy your life in this moment today.*
> > > > . . . >>>>>>>

115

A funny place to start an examination of *interdependence* is by recognizing that our lives begin in a paradoxical state of *dependency* as part of our natural birthright! We began physical life conceived within our mother's womb, and with our first cries, we enter the world in a dependent condition. Infancy requires our being nurtured, supported, taught, encouraged, nourished, sheltered, clothed, protected, defended, taught, and loved unconditionally by others in preparation for growing into a healthy independent person.

Each one of us has received varying degrees of nurturing in vastly differing circumstances. Some may have received excessive overprotection or conversely may have lacked it to the point of neglect or even abandonment. Whether or not you were ideally cared for (whatever *ideally* may be) or experienced serious shortcomings in this area, we all have received at least some minimal level of caring sustenance to have even survived at all. This is where some spiritualists may make the point that our mere survival and existence is proof enough that *the divine* is always overseeing our well-being. While I am not justifying suffering, especially for children, some questions do beckon our exploration. Is there some form of universal intelligence or angelic guardianship that exists, even though our inability to understand suffering makes this hard to believe? Is it conceivable that tragic circumstances help guide each of us on the road to our destiny?

While neither endorsing nor debating such assertions, there are many examples to indicate that even if we have experienced extremely negative conditions in childhood, these experiences can be overcome. In some ways, survivors of such trauma have indicated that they may positively contribute to an important part of our growth. It seems some traumatic accounts have proven to be the fuel that can explosively launch an individual upon their life journey, leading them onto a purposeful path in life. The sad paradox, of course, is that we also observe many tragic tales with little or no obvious positive outcomes.

So is it possible that the imperfect families we are all born into may have been the perfect fit for us in terms of what we were born to experience, to help support our unique lifelong path and our eventual contributions to humanity? To whatever degree our birthparents, adoptive parent, parent figure, or other guardian performed his or her best to provide for us, we have to at least concede that we were all eventually launched alive into our own current orbits. As astronauts have known, entering the atmosphere of our world is always accompanied with great friction that can prove to be a rough and dangerous journey. Yet here on earth, we can grow to consciously create our future as we independently participate and act in the greater human drama of life. Regardless of who your protectors were and how long, how many, or how few of them you depended upon early in life, it is presently irrelevant. We can only proceed in the knowledge that creation and the universe have undeniably cast each of us onto the world stage, at this time and this place! No matter how isolated or difficult our circumstances may now be or once were, at the very least, some level of cosmic care has sustained us to the degree that we remain in this moment to interact with each other in time and space.

Born in dependency, we quite quickly thrust ourselves onto a growing path of independence. Early on all children can be seen expending great energy trying their best to daily learn more and move increasingly forward to do things for themselves. In fact, as soon as a child can talk, you will often here an almost innate demand from toddlers screaming, "Myself, myself!" no matter how hard the task before them is. This is a natural path of development we travel before learning how to create our own joy in this world, as often expressed in our familiar "pursuit of happiness" in declaring our independence.

From my present perspective, I believe that a source of universal power and love exists as an available resource that is never far away. Many traditions have affirmed that this source lies closer than the heartbeat implanted within each of us from our moment of origin. While we may remain unaware of our *own power within*, from my experience, it is there only waiting to be discovered. Comparable to the small acorn where within lies the hidden potential for the immense and miraculous growth of an oak tree, if and when it takes root. Our human potential for growth and creation is unimaginably greater if we but begin to nurture ourselves as adults.

These polar opposite states of *dependence* and *independence* can serve to keep us in a place of healthy equilibrium. To a degree, one might say they provide a sort of equatorial balancing point where life is supported in a temperate zone where we can grow strong and lush. This principle of *balance* helps guide us on our life journey, and it necessarily lies in between harsh extremes. Balance is indeed a healthy ingredient between all the extremes of this world as we know it. Yet the paradox of our world shows us that extremes can also serve a healthy purpose such as the poles controlling seasonal shifts of life on the planet. As humans, we often mirror nature with our personal oscillations that can range from instances of emotional frigidity to the heat of passionate love or from laughter to anger. It seems that opposites are an undeniable part of our human experience and are beneficial if balanced. In contrast, it can be observed that if any extremes are embraced long term as a lifestyle, it can potentially be a dysfunctional trap characterized by a negative dependence, be it forced or freely chosen. On one hand, when these opposing characteristics of being human are used in balance, there seems to be as the song goes, "a time for all things in every season, as the world turns, turns, and turns."

On the other hand, to permanently reside in one extreme or another is an unhealthy invitation for injury and illness. Let's consider, for example, an adult who for whatever reasons never chooses to leave the childlike environment of a parent's supportive home. Perhaps he or she may cling to the security of another's space, essentially choosing to remain in a semidependent existence. Never embarking upon their own journey, they may miss out on the discovery of their destiny and much potential happiness. Obviously, I am only using a generalized example (which is not intended as a judgment of anyone's unique circumstances) to demonstrate an extreme behavior. In the case of our adult remaining in their birth home, it might be analogous to an extended embryonic gestation period. Specifically, the embryonic safety of the womb is positively life supporting, but staying beyond nine months can become detrimental to both baby and mother. The womb is obviously a place intended for only a season, one that balances a healthy *dependence* to support natural growth in preparation for birth on the road to *independence.* Similarly, every emerging adult is invited to embark on their own path of self-discovery, shedding their dependent past and independently choose to enter into an emerging world of interdependence.

This road of independence is one into which we were all born to courageously navigate. It is an opportunity we are offered by our very existence. This, however, is a path that we must necessarily trail blaze to clear the way for the individual development of our own innate talents and interests. Here we can choose to travel forward to discover, understand, proclaim, and experience our unique being, our true self.

It is also worth cautioning that a position of extreme independence can also deliver its own troubles, sometimes characterized by a blind righteousness and destructive self- centeredness. While one may achieve their immediate goals, in its wake, they may discover a barren landscape left behind that is unfit to support their balanced life in the future. (Just look back upon any totalitarian societies to see how a view of excessive *independent separation* played out in the case as it was collectively manifested in Nazi Germany.) Again, in balance, it should be noted that there is no need to singularly vilify Germany as it is not the only nation or culture to err in this way. Over time, it seems every nation and person is tempted to take their turn embracing this affliction at one time or another. Be it fear, righteousness, or other motivation, such exaggerated expressions of individual or societal independence can detrimentally ignore the balance necessary to discover our healthy interrelatedness. Ultimately, it becomes apparent that imbalanced extremes can sacrifice our healthy connection with the lives of other members of our community, human family, and our world at large.

Yet there are positive reasons for the existence of these naturally *dependent* and *independent* aspects of our being. Each possesses benefits that can contribute to living a more balanced and healthy life of *interdependence* together. Such a place of equilibrium is where healing can more fully occur. Understanding this balance provides a portal of sorts for us to enter a personal space where peace awaits all individuals as they recognize we all share a path of common destiny. From this vantage point, we can see that declaring our independence is more effectively established when we integrate a mutually healthy *dependence* upon each other. The paradoxical nature of our freedom requires us to live our unique life while respecting others individuality. In this simultaneous celebration of our human communion, we assert our individuality while supporting positive interaction with one another. The familiar analogy of one body possessing many parts (cells, organs, systems, etc.) to make the whole body function is also a healthy picture for understanding our diversity in the larger world and universe. As the saying goes, it does in fact take all kinds to make the world go round, and that will ever be true.

For these reasons, I propose transcending old paradigms with a new Declaration of Interdependence as a fundamental new principle for uniting peoples, nations, faiths, cultures, and philosophies beyond the previous created boundaries around the earth. This basic understanding could provide a basis for releasing the unbounded potential of even greater individual and institutional independence, while acknowledging a necessary and healthy dependence upon each other. Using this as a guiding principle, I have paraphrased this familiar American document with an updated perspective.

When, in the course of human events, it becomes necessary for a planet of people to dissolve the political bonds which do not positively serve our human family and to assume among the powers of the earth, the separate and equal station to which the laws of nature and of nature's God entitle them, a decent respect to the opinions of humankind requires that they should declare the causes which impel them to end the harmful effects of superficial separation as fellow beings.

We hold these truths to be self-evident, that all men and women are created equal, that they are endowed by their Creator with certain Inalienable rights, and among these are life, liberty, and the pursuit of happiness. That to secure these rights, governments are instituted among men and women, deriving their discretionary powers from the consent of the governed. That whenever any form of government(s) becomes destructive to these ends, it is the right of the people to alter or to abolish it and to institute new government, laying its foundation on such principles and organizing its powers in such form, as to them shall seem most likely to affect their safety and happiness. Prudence, indeed, will dictate that governments long established should not be changed for light and transient causes; and accordingly all experience hath shown that humankind is more disposed to suffer, while evils are sufferable, than to right themselves by abolishing the forms to which they are accustomed.

This can be our *present gift* to each other in every new season of life as we journey onward in each new *present moment.*

All photos by Richard F. Moore

Chapter 6

Family

Understanding Biology and Brotherhood

Be it our immediate biological family or our varied cultural, national, or religious communities, humankind is linked to each other in innumerable ways, most undeniably as part of the greater human family. The term *family* is generally viewed as a naturally conceived and positive unit with the best intentions to foster growth in a helpful and nurturing environment.

    a. Considering the many meanings of family, how might you describe family as being positively helpful?

    b. Conversely, have you ever witnessed a family function (or dysfunction) in unintended ways that have proved negative to its members?

    c. What are some of these dysfunctions?

Answers to such questions can provide some perspective on these units we call a family.

Family might be defined by some in differing contexts such as relations, relatives, kin, ancestors, descendants, lineage, blood line, family tree, breed, village, tribe, clan, nationality, countrymen, religion, or even a continent. Regardless of the positive intentions of these descriptions, it is worth noting how the same terms around family "units" unwittingly serve to separate us from each other. In one case, we might enjoy the warmth of being a family member, and in another, we might feel the cool distancing of being outside the status of family member. In any case, our premise begins with the simple observation that despite any attachment to our own family groupings from birth, we are also reminded of our deeper origin. Whatever genesis story we inherited from our families and traditions, we have undeniably also been born into the human family on planet earth.

Additional insights can also come from studying our biological genealogy or exploring the nature of what we term as brotherhood and sisterhood. Our broader understanding of this can benefit us by exploring the dual vantage points of our physical being alongside our more invisible metaphysical and spiritual relationships that we share together. In either case, the term "family" embraces many meanings and applications worldwide. From biological birthing to bonds of brotherhood, there are many threads that naturally connect us to each other, be it our scientific DNA or our emotional bonding so often demonstrated during times of disasters, natural or manmade. Calamities in the form of typhoons, tsunamis, tornados, or terrorism are examples of emergencies that often reveal our innate empathy and bond with each other. Demonstrations of practical and emotional support are made with an unspoken sense of belonging to the same human family. Help is expressed in many forms outside the apparent limitations of differing languages, religions, or cultural traditions practiced around the globe.

Focusing upon these various familial perspectives, take a moment to reflect upon how family has positively provided for your well-being. Correspondingly, remember those times when we have experienced or observed family dysfunction yielding negative consequences upon our lives. Whether viewing this topic personally or collectively, our understanding of family is an important element for healing during the course of life!

Taking a moment to observe "family" from the realms of science, DNA and genetics is an obvious area of relevance. Less apparent but equally interesting is an exploration within realms of physics. Many studies have produced modern theories that increasingly point to the universe having one source of origin. Whether considering Einstein's theory of relativity, chaos theory, string theory, or M theory (I personally call it mystical theory), or this concept of singularity, we can correlate scientific similarities to many metaphysical and religious accounts. For just a moment then, we will pause from our scientific focus to quickly examine some spiritual traditions for the purpose of comparing creation accounts that might hold some mutual connection similar to the *one source* observations of science.

Hold that thought and try picturing your typical teenager who might react to these "serious" reflections. Imagine their attitude and resulting body language in shaking their head and along with a quick flippant glance (inasmuch as this observation appears so obvious and elementary to them), finally muttering, "Duh, of course, I could have told you that!" Understanding the humorous nature of blatant youthful honesty, we should take heed and also consider this topic from a relatively uncomplicated spiritual perspective. First of all, it is interesting to acknowledge that most every religious tradition has a creation story, be it written or oral. These accounts often contain similar references to a perfect, omnipotent, all-loving, and intelligent creator! Keeping it simple, it is also apparent from most traditions that "in the beginning," we were all created in oneness, in perfect love and harmony together, in a perfect paradise if you will. Continue then with the honesty of our spirited adolescent who is sarcastically responding to adults preoccupied with overanalyzing the simple fact that we are one human family living upon one planet.

This youthful insight and funny quip partially exposes a tragic picture of our human condition when perceived as being separated from God (who created us in the first place) and much of our fellow man outside of our exclusive family unit(s). The simple purity of this teenage remark displays how much of humanity either has forgotten our original oneness or has remained inexplicably unaware of it or, worse yet, has decided to turn a blind eye to that which bonds our human family. As we know, truth can be uttered from the mouths of babes and can also be passionately spoken from the hearts of our adolescents. Within our family structures, what might our young people have to teach adults about healing, family, and spirituality?

When I consider the lifelong love I have for my own family, I can only believe that if God created humanity in perfect love, we must always be destined to receive unconditional love from the creator of the universe. Your response to this question is a critically important answer for everyone's family.

While this book is *not* a religious text per se, for purposes of understanding family, let's examine one more traditional religious viewpoint in helping to contrast more scientific observations. If, for instance, a person embraces the belief that we are all individual parts of one mystical body, each of us a part of a *holy wholeness*, then family must necessarily hold a more inclusive meaning, as expansive as the universe itself. As has been previously pointed out, scientists now understand the moment of creation as having originated from a singular point, where from nothingness the universe emerged in a moment and continues expanding in an ongoing creative process. Scientists themselves hold a healthy awe and reverence of creation as they increasingly document the perfect mathematical synchronization that exists. Despite the many chaotic and explosive forces displayed across the heavens, they often express amazement at an obvious "universal intelligence" at work. Scientists also observe that with each great new discovery, achievement, yielding increased beneficial knowledge, we are always correspondingly presented with ever new questions and challenges, and we discover even more mysteries to address!

Whether one views life from a spiritual or scientific lens, it is obvious that the gift of life and the universe itself are not static but ever changing. Similarly, the paradigms humanity designs are based upon their beliefs of present understanding, yet new discoveries will result in changes that render old beliefs untrue and subsequently require redesigning our old-old paradigms. This process is, of course, no different than when we first discovered the earth was never flat in the first place.

Answers to our very existence may always remain an elusive pursuit of totally satisfying spiritual explanations or ultimate scientific proofs, but the miracle of human life will most likely always remain an ongoing creative process surrounded by an aura of mystery. Just as a baby's birth reveals the inspirational breath of a new life inhaling and exhaling, it mirrors the perfect rhythms observed in the ongoing expansions and contractions of the physical universe. Witness the ebb and flow of the moons cycles and earthly tides or the miracle in the synchronicity of planetary revolutions that contain an incomprehensible order! Science is now pushing the boundaries further, exploring the potential existence of a parallel universe beyond the black holes and the warping of our space-time continuum as we have only recently come to know it.

Having lived the first forty-nine years of my life in the twentieth century, it increasingly feels to me as if the new millennium is culminating in a convergence of science and spirituality. Each discovery sheds new light in developing a picture of a spiritual/physical reality to expose our true oneness. Whether we begin with Genesis, genetics, or the human genome project, all roads may be pointing us toward a heightened pinnacle of common insight, one of a majestic origin from a magnificent singularity, oneness, and our one human family. New knowledge may potentially and mercifully disarm the socially and spiritually charged conflicts that have plagued humankind for centuries. One infamously documented example was during the Renaissance, when popes persecuted scientists and scholars for exposing ancient paradigms as untrue, such as the belief that the sun revolved around the earth. Beyond popes, there were no shortage of other political and religious leaders who also authorized many terrible persecutions to defend the crumbling foundations of their empires under the erroneous belief systems that were now evaporating under the light of new insights.

Now in the new millennium, a growing global awareness continues to rapidly expand as electronic communications and transportation connect us as we have never been before. These twenty-first-century circumstances possess the potential for an historical spiritual and scientific convergence, and present us with an opportunity to harmoniously embrace what we have in common. Such a seismic shift could positively reconstruct the cornerstones of our world's oldest civilizations upon healthy and firmer foundations. Can we dare seize this moment to constructively build a healthier understanding of our humanity? Newly evolving global paradigms need not be feared and need not contradict or invalidate any positive lessons that past traditions have to teach us.

It often appears to me that the world's contradictions and paradoxes merely reflect the awesome diversity of billions of unique individuals living upon the planet together. The sometimes apparent chaos of this diversity may just reveal to us the perfection of our collective gifts to each other as a human family. Yes, both scientifically and religiously, everything under creation seems to have its place. All of life's opposites in the physical world are blessed; each is an equally divine part of creation when understood in their balanced purposes. Contemplating the nature of opposites one can see life from up or down, right or left, hot or cold, in or out, above or below, and so on. In the end, all perspectives have an undeniable function and place in the design and balance to support all of life.

I do not write with the authority (or the bias) of a theologian, scientist, academic, or expert in any of these fields; I am limited in comprehensively addressing these mysteries. I do, however, write from the depths and power of my own experiences and observations. From this vantage point, I have clearly witnessed that the expression of *love* (giving and receiving) is a key element essential to any family's purpose and thus a critical ingredient for healing.

In the context of our own life path then (and by any definition of family), *love* is obviously what helps any relationship function more beautifully in overcoming the stresses that naturally accompany growth and development at any stage of life. By mutually ministering and caring for each other, love can indeed conquer all, curing us no matter how difficult our problems or how tragic our past outcomes. In contrast, the lack of love can foster dysfunctions exponentially harmful to all. Family functionality at any level professes positive intentions to form bonds of love that support growth and independence to pursue the basic of purposes in life such as

- providing food, shelter, and clothing, while emotionally nurturing our healthy growth
- educating, with mutual teaching and learning
- fostering the freedom to experience any aspects of life between birth and physical death
- consciously manifesting love to spontaneously share in the joy of life in each new moment; and
- nourishing individual growth, blessing each member to discover their personal destiny.

When we fail to bring love into any type of family, we unwittingly distance ourselves from each other and our purpose, and we diminish our source of strength. Here we risk creating an illusion of our own making, a dead-end road that silently separates us from our healthy path and ultimate destination. Be heartened, however, for in the end, these are only imagined detours delaying us. Eventually, we can elect to find our way back to our own path, on that proverbial *highway to heaven*. While we may view such dysfunctional twists and turns in the road as regrettable mistakes or errors, they can also serve us as potentially beneficial experiences. In looking back, it is simply not healthy to spend time in judging any right or wrong. It is never truly necessary or productive beyond acknowledgement of your decision to change a pattern you no longer choose to repeat. In the end, we can simply decide to use our free will to rediscover and express love more fully.

For some additional perspective on this matter of judging things as right or wrong, let's consider a historical account of difficulties incurred during Lewis and Clark's exploration of the American West. Would one negatively summarize this expedition as predominately full of mistakes when, in fact, their travels and observations ultimately contributed to a valuable new base of beneficial knowledge? Whether intended or not, their journey proved productive in many ways, just as are our own imperfect life experiences can help guide us forward by remembering our connection to the human family and our one source. This source always resides within us, and we can learn to use it as our internal GPS (as Lewis and Clark must have also listened to their "inner voice" with faith and courage) in finding the salvation of our real nature. This is also our quiet but powerful internal focal point and available to us for personal healing at all times.

Over time, I have gradually come to incorporate meditation and quiet prayer for guidance within my own immediate family as well as guiding me with the larger connection with my fellow beings. Here I reflected upon broken examples of family, including just one of my ancestral homelands where ancient tribal Celtic families once dwelled together. Their state of sectarian division (and subsequent failure to love each other) has gradually and tragically played out for centuries in Northern Ireland. As the world has seen, such a disconnection or separation of family can lead to untold sadness and grief. Mercifully, recent developments have begun to foster healing as individuals begin to acknowledge how each other's collective pain was repeatedly inflicted upon all divisions in a useless cycle of "evening the score." A similarly divisive example is also recognizable with our Jewish and Palestinian brothers and sisters who are in reality distant cousins in human history. (DNA documentation will ultimately chart out every ones genetic relationship to each other on humanity's family tree.) Within our hearts, we already sense this to be true, with or without scientific proof.

These infamous examples can help provide insights on how love needs to first be chosen individually in our own hearts before it can be better cultivated into our family units. If we as a human family are to return to our promised land, a critical mass of courageous individuals must first act to invite one person at a time back to the table of brotherhood and sisterhood. Naturally, it is up to each one of us, as creation will always honor our individual freedom to choose either way. Will we continuing choosing to maintain our current conflicts, or will we begin creating a more inclusive future together as a human family? It will remain up to each one of us to consciously act upon this choice that is only yours to make. Such is the nature of an unconditionally loving creator, always honoring our freedom to choose in our own time! Hence, wherever one is at in their journey through life, you always remain free to access your power within or not.

A concluding thought worth noting is that some scientists are hypothesizing that a parallel universe may possibly exist that allows alternative realities to exist simultaneously. Could this possibly mirror some religious accounts of a second coming, or a 'rapture' where individual free will choices are consciously and collectively manifested? Differing outcomes in different places? In the loving context of our paradoxically human-divine family, it is an interesting reflection where one may someday choose living in harmony, or continue to live on in the current human paradigm where we are separated from a creator.

"We allow our ignorance to prevail upon us and make us think we can survive alone, alone in patches, alone in groups, alone in races, even alone in genders" (Maya Angelou).

Brotherhood/Sisterhood

Brother Sun, Sister Moon,
Father Time, Mother Earth,
Deliver us, and make it soon,
Guide us to our own rebirth.

Women and men, would you be so kind,
To bless each other, renewing humankind.
Brother, sister, father, and mother,
Bestowing new blessings upon each other,
Blesses the nature of our interdependence.
For liberty loves all, our true independence.

In concluding our many considerations of family units from small and large, biological and beyond, the following personal notes and poems of this chapter are offered to help intuitively guide our sense

of family in a positive direction. The reflections are presented in the following:

A. The Family of My Youth

B. My Adult Family

C. Our Greater Human Family

1. The Family of My Youth

Born in 1951, the third of nine children, I grew up with three younger sisters and five brothers. My father was a machinist working for a large corporation, and my mom was one who proudly affirmed that her chosen vocation was motherhood. Over time, I would learn she had once deeply desired to be a nurse, but like many women at that time, she was not afforded the opportunity to pursue further education. Mom was the daughter of an Irish immigrant woman who raised her in a very strict Roman Catholic tradition. While this maternal grandmother of mine may have been traditional in one sense, she must have also been a radically courageous individual. As a nineteen-year-old woman, she had fled her native Ireland, boarding a boat bound for the USA *alone* around 1900 to take a job as a maid in a mansion in Buffalo, New York.

A half century later, I was born into the now infamous baby boom generation. The 1950s included many strange contradictions of stability and prosperity (truer for white males than most others), alongside many societal problems just coming to a boil below the surface of polite society. Post–World War II patriotism is now well documented for its communist paranoia demonstrated by the ironic blacklisting its "free-speaking citizens." It was also public policy to detonate atomic *test* bombs on American soil while aggressively promoting the building of bomb shelters in every community. In contrast to this prevailing environment of fear, we also felt safe, secure, and loved within our homes. While being well fed, sheltered, and cared for in a positive manner, we were also being indoctrinated with many prevailing pathologies characteristic of those times. They included both religious and political orthodoxies which in general made life considerably more difficult for any minority group. Most notably were issues denying obvious civil rights, depriving women of freedoms, and violent persecution for sexual orientations to name a few. Nevertheless, life for the mainstream majority of post WWII citizens was prosperous by most standards. Then came the

1960s, and the pressure cooker boiled over! Forces on many fronts shattered foundations in and out of the home.

On a more personal level, *security* (however that may be defined as) seemed as if it were a birthright in my 1950s childhood. This would all cave in for me in the '60s culminating in 1969 when my dad died suddenly from a stroke at a mere fifty years of age. My dear mom was left with the daunting task of keeping all nine of us together amid a growing insecurity now casting a long shadow on our family. The overwhelming uncertainty would impact each member of our family in powerfully different ways. It became revealing over time as each sibling expressed their own reflections, memories, and unique experiences in dealing with loss.

Just two years later, when Mom was getting her grip on life back, my thirteen-year-old brother was accidentally killed in another one of those senseless shootings from kids playing with a neighbor's hunting rifle. Words still cannot ever capture the deep sadness from these two tragic losses. After everything is said and done, the process of growing up in any family is not always pretty. Accepting this, one can better understand the benefits and detriments that occur in the lives of everyone's unique family experiences. I believe any healing around family lies in our ability to look back and give the benefit of the doubt that our parents or guardians did the best they knew how in getting us into adulthood alive. In appreciation of this, the following poems offer snapshots from some of my family experiences including moments of weakness and strength, loss and love, and the joy in living each day fully! Hopefully, they possess some universal family resonance.

"A FatherLess Moore"

Why, young man, do you appear so sad?
Thy eyes cast down, seeing only gray and bad.
What torture torments this growing lad?
With youth in hand, a time to be colorful and glad!

Goodbye this morning, with only a wave to his dad,
By midday they informed him of a loss he now had!
So you see his sadness, the reason he cried,
With memories Engraved, he grieves his Dad died.

Never to be the same, never to be seen,
Happiness to restore, a memory to glean,
If only I had known, or could have foreseen,
I would have hugged harder, at age seventeen!

Where are you now, oh, father, my father?
Sometimes you seem, so distant and farther
Though looking back, I sensed you were near,
As trials and troubles did slowly disappear!

Like clouds with each passing, the skies do clear,
Revealing heavenly insights, healing my fear.
As my vision improved, I envisioned you here,
Our destiny reveals, we are eternally dear.

Rebirthing from an Obituary's Death

He was alive, living life fully,
Sharing himself, enjoying it wholly
Engaged in the lives of so many beings
Receiving their love, respecting their feelings.

He mutually transmitted to others
That same energy to live as brothers,
Enjoying all of life, in love,
He lives though stilled, while we still live!

In our mourning we give new birth,
By accounting for his life of worth,
Mysteriously this old spirit spawns,
His insights live on, as a new age dawns.

Internally questioning all earthly reasoning,
We bury the emotions from deaths dark sting.
Experiencing deep loss in the starkest season,
The human spirit lives beyond mere logic or reason!

The Smile

In our frightening moment of loss and need,
Both body and spirits you stopped to feed.
You nourished us but did not speak,
As our family lay so weary and weak.

Descending into our vertigo view,
You did not spin religious perspective.

Complexions were restored to a healthy hue,
As smiles were sown and lovingly reflective.

Smiling continues when remembering the numerous kindnesses given during
a time of need.

(I was fortunate I chose to present this poem to my mother, just several
months before she succumbed to cancer.)

MATERNALLY OURS, ETERNALLY YOURS

You lent us an ear, and quelled our fear,
A mother so dear, you were always there!
A chosen vocation, chose with elation,
Freely desiring to give birth, in harmony with mother earth.
With a willing spirit of limitless sharing,
Mom was there healing and caring!

In the winter we were warmed in many a way,
Through the long cold nights, until the new day.
In nurturing us, she both clothed and fed,
From mornings sunrise, until tucked in bed.
One day healthy, the next sickly infected,
Children were loved, healed, and protected.

While reading to us our favorite book,
It came alive as she gave a certain look,
Her voice made the story remarkably real,
Imprinting on us, that books held an appeal.
Yes she was there to teach and to read,
But she also was there in an hour of need!

In good times and bad,
She was ready to share,
Giving what she had
Mom always was there!

In the springtime she taught gardening,
Teaching healthy growth, to someday sow our seed.
When wronged she taught pardoning,
And that redemption we would need.
The Eastern sun, we saw it rising so clear,

There she was again, in the spring of our year.
She cooked and cleaned,
She nursed and shopped,
She ironed and then leaned,
Until in bed we all dropped.

Little energy was left for a mother to spare,
Except to be present, in sleep she was there!
In the dog days of summer it could be apparent,
On the toll life could take, in the tests of a parent.
As kids we would take our turns feeling blue,
In a world so coarse, where we harshly grew.
Nevertheless, in the heat of the day,
A mother was there, in work and play.

Wiping our tears, she eased our fear,
Her voice cheery, she was ever near!
Please Lord our petitions do hear,
In her needy hour, now lift her fear!

In the autumn of this task,
Befalls a fatigue, rest assured,
But leaves could never mask,
A satisfaction that pleasured.
An abundant harvest she now measured,
Of the young adults she now treasured.
Again she was there, to witness what she started,
And was blessed to see it before she departed.

Now lend me your ear,
Let me quell your fear,
Listen, Mom, and you will hear,
Mutual love will always be near.
To explain illness and death,
One cannot reconcile the reasons,
So with my life giving breath,
I proclaim you a Mother for all seasons.

Photo by Richard F. Moore

A relevant footnote as to the extent of my mother's caring for all *family* and how it extended outwardly. Despite the rigors of raising nine children, she volunteered to host exchange students for months at a time from Spain, France, Ecuador, and Japan. Recognize that the 1940s and 1950s household did not offer the many benefits of today's mechanized conveniences, as daily life required the hand wringing of laundry, drying clothes outdoors, and laboriously cooking everything from scratch and much more. Through her church involvement, she also welcomed several young women into our home for extended stays. I would learn later that these were adolescent girls from various East Coast cities who had either been pregnant and or suicidal. As a youngster, I knew none of this, but I only remember enjoying the company of our guests by cooking, playing games with them, and just laughing as if they were just another family member. For a time, they were, and I firmly believe it was my mom's conscious intent to give us a real sense of belonging to the human family!

****

2. My Adult Family

Be it our immediate family (biological or otherwise), we are undeniably linked to nurturing and healing each other in innumerable ways. Some related reflections as a father of three.

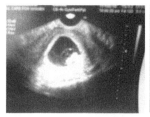

A child from nowhere, embraced by two,
Regardless of gender, happy with any hue.
Born a conception, of incomparable truth,
From newborn, to toddler, and into youth.

Obviously simple, complex to comprehend,
A life is beginning, here on without end.
A breathtaking birth, in giving first breath,
Miracle mother earth, bears life from death.

In the normal course of our daily life,
Comes a healthy dose of discord and strife.
Shades of blue and gray, so plain to see,
A child brings balance, laughter and glee.

Labored by love; busy, tired and drained,
Constant energy, on this child to be trained.
The pleasure of parenting, while not all joy,
Invites us to lavish, loving girl or boy!

Weathering the tough times, and rougher rains,
Growth is born in darkness, of loss and deep pains!
Yet harvesting growth is a pleasure supreme,
Transforming each tear, to nourish a dream.

3. Our Greater Human Family: Recognizing Our Global Village.

Daughters

The dawning of creation,
Creation's gracious gift,
Truth is the daughter of all time.

A spawning of nations, spanning the globe,
Adopting us into this world,
We adapt to her rhythmic time.

Adept at loving, our daughters thus give,
Birthing divine expressions, nurturing souls to live.
So great a creation, God's physical embracing,
With divine emanations, via daughterly manifestations.

For every daughter created, I adopt as if she were mine,
So grand is a daughters gracing, a Father's gift for all of time.

Sibling Gifts
(To Matt & Laurel)

In a brother's leaving, a sister became bound,
As through her grieving, a life of love was found.
Extending her touch, one now understands,
Renewed relationships, form a loving heart and hands.
Sacred and secure, her love uplifts,
A hearts healing cure, born of sibling gifts.

Abundance

Friends, men, and women of our human family,
Bend me your ears in heartfelt palpability.
In the present hour of global sharing,
Our spheres of love, influence caring.

Such a sacred space to visit and stand,
Where two talk, touching heart and hand
For such solo roles we will happily bless,
An addition of friends shares equalness.

Our soul guides our lives into a renewed bliss,
Stronger and more positive in all relationships.
Knowing we share in love's creative lessons,
Loving more, not less in unlimited expressions.

Not insecure with suspect scarcity,
But assured of an ever expanding infinity.
Each balanced expression of light and love,
Observe the two-winged flight of the dove.

Creating more love in universal sight,
Just as stars create new heat and light.
A newly ignited lighthearted sharing,
Delighted by Love, laughing, and caring.

One gesture of love is not an expenditure,
But a growing investment for love to endure,
To further feed all with renewable abundance,
Souls quenched by love's welcome redundancy.

One of us, two, and all of humankind,
Desire a renewed loving state of mind.
Like powerful water harnessed into electricity,
Love generates our ever expanding capacity.

So pass it on, by embracing it today,
By touching others along life's way.
Giving your love, frees you to grow,
Lighting the way with your radiant glow.

Circulate nourishment for the human heart,
Our natures are divine, and not really apart.
A fresh breath inspires substantive sharing,
Our human family, loving, laughing, and caring.

Reflections for Healing
(Your Optional Journal)

Chapter 6
Family
Understanding Biology and Brotherhood

What reflections of your own personal family came to mind in this chapter?

A. Family of your youth?

B. Your own adult family?

Do you have thoughts (positive or negative) on your connection to any larger sense of family outside of personal biological relationships?

Did you have any other perspectives that you might choose to further explore?

Can you identify any paradigms that, if reshaped, might help positively connect the many family groupings that exist around our world?

Did any poetic mediation(s) on the theme of family prove insightful or helpful in any way?

Your Other Notes:

Chapter 7

Illumination

Understanding Love and Light

I recall the joy of writing poetry since my middle-school years, but over time, I regrettably lost or discarded these youthful writings just as I would later part with my outdated vinyl records during my midlife years. In 2010, I had occasion to say hello to an old friend living out of state whom I had known since composing those middle-school verses. Somehow we had both managed to keep up some intermittent contact over the busy decades of raising our families. Unfortunately, the occasion for seeing her was to attend a memorial service for her mother who had recently passed away. We had a pleasant but sobering chat at the occasion, before a hug goodbye.

A short time later, I received a lovely follow-up letter from her. She informed me that I had once given her a poem of friendship back in 1965 after her family had relocated from Texas to Niagara Falls, where we attended school together. I had long forgotten about it, but when she mailed me the verses, I began recalling my poem and could not help but smile.

In brief, her purpose was to encourage my desire to write this book on healing, and she wanted me to know my poem had traveled with her for over forty years. She explained that my simple words of encouragement to her in 1965 would continue to remind her of her essential value over many decades and some seven cities she would subsequently call home. I will share with you the closing verse I once wrote at fourteen years of age, followed by her comments from the letter she sent in 2010.

In 1965 I wrote:

> *My friend, I sincerely mean all that I say*
> *And I hope it will help you in some form or way,*
> *For when I see you it raises my spirit,*
> *So embrace your unique value, and truly hear it.*

Forty-five years later, she corresponded back and wrote:
>*Yes, your poem helped me in an amazing way as I carried it with me to work every day all these decades.*
>*The past is over, it's all said and done yet you're still in my life as a precious friend. Amazing!*
>*Thank you for everything you have shared with me.*

She concluded her handwritten letter, encouraging me to write and publish my book of poetry for others to reflect upon. You can bet it brought a tear to my eyes, and it affirmed my desire to finish this book. After delays from my heart attack and my wife's strokes, *onward we proceeded!*

The prose in this chapter are intended to be beautiful by their symbolic brevity. Such is the nature of any revelation when love and light illuminate what is important and reduce the need for too many words to describe what is ultimately indescribable*!*

Like the deceptions hidden in any darkness, words can also be inadequate in their ability to express the light within our spirits. Despite the clever and magical illusions that the blackness of night presents to us by concealing light, the sun conversely exposes all that was hidden from our eyes to clearly view once again. Similarly, in our lives, there are those corresponding interpersonal bright spots that dawn upon us in amazing moments to shine on our lives and our relationships. It may be a friend, family member, business associate, total stranger, or stranger yet, a nameless or homeless person who just comes out of the blue and into our presence. At such times, we mutually intersect for a potentially purposeful moment; but only if we are paying attention?

In just one immeasurable moment, we can be touched, smiled upon, listened to, inspired, or moved in such a way as to shift the entire focus of your life or equally impact the lives of others. Refocusing the lens of our lives to permit more light, we may provide greater clarity with enhanced foresight. This experience can occur instantly, beyond the speed of light, surpassing our usual eyesight, while transcending any humble words we may utter.

In these special moments we can sense and feel the miracle for which we were created to be and appreciate life with all our innate senses. By the way, whoever proved there are only X number of senses? (Rudolf Steiner, an Austrian philosopher, social reformer, and architect, once lectured on "Man's Twelve Senses in Their Relationship to Imagination, Inspiration, and Intuition.")

Such moments can mercifully remind us to notice the childlike magic that is ever before us to illuminate our lives with love and intuitively guide our personal and collective path in life. This says much about our journey along life's ongoing pathway. As our *observations* lead us to gain new *perspectives* and deeper *understandings*, we grow in wisdom, and grace to attain a peace that transcends words. As we gain fresh insights about life as we previously knew it, we will all contribute to forming positive new paradigms for humanity to further flower

Recognizing the limitations of language, I do hope the poetry below effectively speaks to our hearts by transcending my humble words, just as it did to my friend who has now kept my heartfelt poem for over fifty years. So it is I forge ahead striving to express the truth of my own while still walking this earth, in the hopes of illuminating someone's life before my leaving. May it serve to brighten our pathways along the road to our inevitable bright future together and shine our light upon the way to our healthy destiny.

Torchlight

One holds it high, with heart aflame,
Lighting the night sky, striking love's name.
Life flows with confidence in stride and pace.
Running over and coupling the human race.

In absence of ego, a source of our false pride.
Moving ever forward or stepping aside,
A torchlight shines a light to lead,
The first and last, and all the accompanied.

This beacon guides our limited human sight,
Each arriving in their own time of flight.
With a passionate sigh, and hearts ablaze,
Lighting our world, blesses nights and days.

Brushstrokes Envisioned

Your words paint an impression upon thee,
With each gentle stroke you elegantly brush,
Using strands of silken hair, you colorfully reshape me;
Hues give expression, as an image grows lush.

Mirrors simply reflect our complexity,
Of two enjoined in social intercourse,
Every path arrives at destinations differently,

Yet from the same energy of original force.
Indeed who knows of any future travels,
Or predestinations, when fate unravels.

Painting a picture in which we care,
Content with a vision we will once again meet.
With relevant writings created to share.
Always at peace whenever we next greet.

We will speak more of these tomorrows,
With inspired strokes we erase old sorrows,
When we brush away today's concerns,
We present new moments to love and learn.

Celebration

Into our being the seed of love is sown,
Engaging others, our spirits have grown.
Gifting two into one, as you now integrate
Enjoying each moment, you will thus create.

No longer living on solely singular needs,
An interdependent soul fully succeeds.
Love is a gift given in a spirit so free,
That it frees your spirits to simply be.

A season of peace, fully overcoming separation,
A reason we share joyfully in your celebration.
So accept this expression, we happily bestow,
We share in your love, as it continues to grow.

Love's Reign

Searching for a land where love may reign.
Securing salvation for the soul to reclaim.

Inheriting hollow answers over the years.
Sorrow drops a spirit in the form of tears,
Drenched with sadness in a drowning rain,
Our Souls Seek love, echoing a hearts refrain.

Richard Francis Moore

Hoping for freedom from fear and shame,
Searching for a land where love may reign.

In fear and shame, a soul screams out,
A primal query, as it wanders about,
For whom, why, and what on earth for?
Madness is born from a false fervor.

Clinging to our minds, our sanity to maintain,
Onward we walk to where love might reign.

In anguish, the human heart earnestly asks,
It prays for the truth, unveiling our egos masks,
To discover its own truth, in performing its task.

Exhausted in searching beyond outward reach,
Looking inward, a begging soul does beseech,
Yielding joyful sounds, replacing normal speech.

Created to love fully and freely, our heavenly design,
Recognizing our unity, reflecting all as divine.
In experiencing our true nature, we now maintain,
Birthright of a loving world, our inherited domain.

The soul is eternally free to sing loving refrains,
Being divine truth, understanding love always reigns.

Photo by Richard F. Moore

I am a person whose life experiences and spiritual path have been positively enhanced by various aspects of every major religious tradition. In respecting all creation and all people, I share in good faith a repetitive dream that continued recurring for me over many years. In the year 2000, this dream had repeatedly awakened me one winter's night with the same persistent message. At the time, I just discounted it as that same old dream and refused to take it too seriously. What was different this time was the repetition throughout the same night. After the third recurrence, I could not get back to sleep, so I eventually left my bed for the computer and decided to write down these unrelenting communications. I later returned to bed for a peaceful sleep after placing a copy in my files where it remained largely forgotten for over a decade until my writing this book. The content of my old notes read:

Let it be known that the divine speaks to *everyone*, from within. Some are spoken to through dreams, visions, angels, science, and a myriad of other channels so innumerable as to be beyond our comprehension. At this time in human history, *everyone* is being individually alerted and invited to prepare for receiving each other in a renewal of love, faith, and unity. This will also present a collective opportunity for the world's religious institutions to demonstrate spiritual truth by example, thereby fulfilling their professed potential and original purpose for having come into existence in the first place.

Governmental and institutional conflicts of interests aside, this is primarily a calling for each individual to hear. The brief message is intuitively listen within and then live in the knowledge that no longer does one need to die for one's faith, country or any cause. The future is now ours to bring to fruition by becoming aware of your birthright. You were created to produce peace in abundance and are now called to reclaim your inheritance, and enjoy the paradise of your past.

If you so choose, you have the free will to remain in your current fearful state of being. The choice has always been yours. A new paradigm of loving unity awaits and welcomes anyone who freely claims this future as realized.

The following poem was inspired by this dream.

Religions Renewal

Go back before that original sin,
Back to our creation as related kin.
Before any philosophical treatise or theology,
Prior to words, with voluminous Christology.
Before patriarchal clerics banned science as revolution,
Burning healers as heretics, and books on evolution.

When did you cease believing in omnipotence?
Who limited your God to speak to only one faith?
God's unlimited power speaks to all without wrath,
With messengers to the masses, on every cultures path.
Unconditional love, without reasons or recompense,
Love produces sweet fruits, faithful to common sense!

Real renewal, restores us wholly in communion,
May religion now reembrace our loving reunion,
Rise up from lying in your state of original sin,
remembering your inheritance of eternal origin!

Turn away from the paradigm you call sin,
Recall your birthright, of divine power within.

A Soldier's Uprising"

Who dares to speak for the dead?
Especially for the deceased soldier?
If they had ceased the firing to avoid the grave,
Could they shed light on war in the home of the brave?

Would they raise a voice for freedom for their offspring?
Free from death, destruction, and a life of grieving?
Could they now give new birth to new resolutions?
Healing earth and man with sustainable solutions?

We listen with lament as the survivors speak,
With familiar eulogies, death continues to wreak.
In the name of honor, multiplying death,
Body counts rising, justifying their last breath.

Condemning generations to an embattled ending,
In a life of brevity, they will die young defending.
How long to secure a just and lasting peace?
In disregarding life, death denies our release!

So if our dead soldiers arose this day,
What on earth would they convey?
Embracing family and comrade, while healing the sad?

Would they next advise us to keep up the good fight?
To stay the course or perhaps a different insight?
With the centuries of war in historical hindsight,
Would their rising turn the tide, with fresh foresight?

Never ask the politician or preacher,
Not the newsman nor the teacher,
For each plays their role, in scripted words they cast,
As each soldier is buried, their talk silences our past.
What might a soldier have spoken, would it be surprising?
If they could speak their peace during a soldiers uprising?

This tragic play, buries a truth so olden,
I pray some general arises to embolden,
Citizens and soldiers to invade new ground,
To conquer a peace, that can be wrested or found.
Who possesses the courage to rise up and speak?
Truly honoring their sacrifices, with new solutions we seek.

Soaring

Ever seeking new perspective,
Soaring swift and confident in your flight,
If for only one moment so reflective,
You were able to reach new heights.

Finding comfort in each moment and place.
Trusting in the spreading of our wings,
Spanning both time and physical space,
Breathtakingly inspired, exhaling voices sing,

In effortless flight, an uplifting energy,
A wonderful sight of collective synergy.

So spread your positive nature,
The sharing of goodwill,
Inherent in each loving creature,
In love, exercising your free will.

Your spirit is lightened and elevated,
Seeing through the darkest mourning,
Longing for love is no longer belated,
Elevated to our natural state of soaring.

Artwork by Jimi Tutko

Reflections for Healing
(Your Optional Journal)

Chapter 7
Illumination
Understanding Love and Light

What observations caught your attention in this chapter? Did any lightbulbs go off for you?

Did you gain any new perspectives that you might choose to further explore?

Did you garner any new insight in regard to possible new paradigms regarding the future roles for our religious, social, and political institutions?

Did any poetic mediation prove insightful or helpful in any way?

Your Other Notes:

Chapter 8

Healing

Understanding Forgiveness and Freedom

Grant that I may not so much seek to be consoled, as to console.
It is in pardoning that we are pardoned.
—*Prayer of Francis of Assisi*

Biographical Briefing

Chronologically advancing into my midfifties, I found my peace of mind was increasingly disturbed in regard to escalating global conflicts begging for an equivalent need for global healing. Despite the wealth of positive technological advancements, particularly in communications, worldwide, these tensions continue to grow in scope with greater violence and increasing poverty. I began to give fresh thought to our global conditions while drawing upon the words of the many world leaders I had been so privileged to see and hear speak in person in recent years.

Reflecting upon the substance of their observations, I began trying to identify their most significant messages, those that left a lasting impression upon me. To my great surprise, I decided that former British prime minister Tony Blair's remarks contained some of the more revealing observations based upon his experience in relation to healing. He subtly addressed themes of forgiveness (an unusual focus for a former politician) necessary for humanity to gain freedom from our often self-made dilemmas. As I had noticed with other political speakers, once they were out of elective office, most of them were more relaxed and increasingly candid, possessing an honesty that was seemingly lacking when they occupied their positions of power. Accordingly, Mr. Blair positively astounded me with his clarity on topics critical to all of humankind.

So it was on the evening of October 7, 2009, that he shared many observations, but his most gripping story concerned the fragile experience of working together over several years with both Protestant and Catholic leaders in Northern Ireland. He and others would give renewed energy to this old conflict in the great hope of creating a breakthrough that could bring about an opportunity for all peoples of that region to freely choose a

148

path of peace, leaving behind a stagnant paradigm that maintained a legacy of hatred, distrust, and cyclical violence!

To be very brief, he shared background information on the many ups and downs of this road offering an invitation to help design the possibility of new beginnings of peace. He spoke of many critical and courageous moments by individuals at first, followed eventually by groups on all sides of the conflict.

Mr. Blair highlighted a particular exchange that eventually proved a breakthrough in establishing some genuine connections with each other. With a stated intention of establishing respect for all, they gently began with building the smallest benefit of the doubt to operate with some measure of trust, fragile as it no doubt was.

Specifically, he explained that all parties had agreed beforehand to conduct a meeting with a defined format to simply build understanding. The approach required that two persons from each side of the conflict would take turns explaining their deepest hurt, pain, agony, or injustice that they and their families had suffered at the hands of their political-sectarian opposition. This was to be done without interrupting the person speaking, with a promise to keep one's ears open and truly just listen. The goal was ever so simple but incredibly heavy hearted; the other person needed not only to listen but also, upon conclusion, to acknowledge the speaker and let that person know they actually understood the reasons for his or her long-suffering hurt and anger. In essence, they had preagreed to stand in the other person's shoes for a moment for the sole purpose of understanding their circumstances; no one needed to agree or disagree with anyone else.

The process was then reversed as roles required that speaking and listening now go in the other direction. Given their professed religious convictions, they were now all relying on the best of each other's spiritual moorings to earnestly and prayerfully continue this emotionally charged and grievously painful exercise. The desperate hope was to bridge some initial sense of comprehension (not agreement) and acknowledgment of the suffering incurred from each other's perspectives. The desired outcome was to establish a baseline foundation of trust and respect, if any reconciliation was ever to take place.

He happily reported that this approach had succeeded in establishing a miraculous breakthrough, and though it was fragile and subtle, it did create a serious and hopeful new beginning. He later relayed that since he left office as prime minister, he was now trying to use this experience from Northern Ireland and apply these healing lessons elsewhere, adding that he agreed to serve as a United Nations' special peace envoy to the Israeli-Palestinian conflict.

Since hearing him that evening, I could not help but consider the potential for such principles to be used to benefit others in our world, such as America's overdue need to reach out to Native American populations and respectfully recognize their sufferings to begin a process of healing all citizens. This one example of a healthy new beginning can help us recognize and honor each other and our richly different cultures while acknowledging a tragic history of ignorance and misunderstanding. Only when there is understanding and acknowledgment can we hope to arrive at forgiveness, and therein always lies our world's hope for experiencing true freedom. By understanding many perspectives, we all stand to gain more wisdom, thereby growing in liberty and justice for all! I, for one, have grown in appreciation of our brilliant American Declaration of Independence and Constitution as visionary documents expressing the desire for human freedom. Despite these historic documents, the tragic irony remains that they were written at a time predominated by black slavery, Native Indian genocide, and limited rights for women. Yet the seeds of greater liberty and freedom were sown in these documents, and they continue to germinate to this day. The architects of these new governing documents of proved revolutionary in many ways, expressing universal feelings felt by individuals around the world, many of whom would immigrate in the centuries to follow. This was a radical departure from the old world paradigms supporting monarchies, dictatorships, and political theocracies as demonstrated in the longstanding inquisition led by the Catholic Church. A significant new paradigm had taken root in the new world of America.

(Once again, this book is neither a religious text nor an agnostic or scientific thesis. I utilize references from all of these paradigms solely because they are familiar to everyone and have brought our world to where it is today.)

Proceeding against this backdrop, I once again found myself increasingly disrupted from my sleep at night. Many consistent messages were contained in these recurring dreams, this time from a spirit claiming to speak from "the highest authority." *No*, I have never heard any audible voice, but I only had a common dreamlike experience. The only unusual aspect to this was the unrelenting nature of its annoying repetitive pattern. These went on for many weeks, repeatedly paraphrasing a theme that "We are not going to hell . . . despite the fact we have been freely choosing to create a living hell for ourselves for a long time now. Humankind continues to project man made attributes upon creation with many inferences and ungodly perceptions as suggested below.

- God has limitations, such as only communicating through one religion.
- There exists a scarcity of resources in the universe.
- God is an angry and jealous deity, therefore not unconditionally loving.
- We have been cast off and punished, thus being separated from our source of creation.
- We must further fear the threat of eternal punishment.
- Mankind's almost religious commitment to a paradigm of (a self-fulfilling apocalyptic prophecy) war and annihilation is *not* inevitable and is not spiritual.
- Prophesies were not intended as predetermined fates, but are a guide to aid the human heart in freely choosing to co-create a divine future together.

"Let it be known that by maintaining these ungodly thoughts, humanity will continue to manifest similarly tragic results they so long as they reaffirm such false beliefs. The documented histories of every culture, nation, and religion are all sadly incriminated for their tragic violence as competing groups. No longer believe these ideas—they are false concepts and untrue representations of your true human and divine nature!"

Again, I generally did not give these dreams any serious thought. (It is not my nature to take such things to heart, let alone take myself too seriously.) But over time, these themes grew more relevant and quite naturally found expression into my poetry. During this time, I had also begun reading many books from a wide array of authors who reaffirmed many of these thoughts I was dreaming of. Additionally, these concepts were being echoed by the many nurses and complementary healers whom I was professionally interviewing at the time. Eventually, I could no longer ignore the unrelenting dreams, all similar and all restating these themes in various ways.

Let me be clear in asserting that I do *not* portray myself or present my dreams as possessing any special mystical connection as I am predisposed to assume that like most others, my dreams simply come from my own feelings and reflect the times in which I live. We all absorb new information or new revelations, if you will, daily. Be it scientific or spiritual, I believe we are all spoken to with divine inspirations if we but utilize our incredible human capacities to quietly listen. After all, it is logical to believe that a creator can speak to us through all of creation, and in this sense, divine communication is both miraculous, normal, and available to everyone. None of us being more or less special than the next, we should also listen more closely as we speak with each other.

Along these lines, I'd share that since becoming a father at twenty-eight years of age, I established a practice of beginning my day by reading a prayerful meditation with a brief quiet period before entering into the noise of the day. During reflection one morning, I finally decided to scribe the messages of these dreams I was having into my computer.

In a subsequent meditation, I considered how these ancient constructs have influenced historical law and the resulting punitive practices we have witnessed to this day. Around much of the globe, we can observe how most societies were essentially designed within various religious traditions with one predominant premise being that punishing people was an effective way to help prevent future hellish human behaviors. Arguably, these are largely patriarchal initiatives that have objectively never attained their desired preventative intentions! I respectfully acknowledge and understand that some people still believe things would be even worse without the existence of our societies "just punishments." So as not to waste energy and time arguing the righteousness of any pros or cons nor to get bogged down in the mire of religious semantics, let each reader simply consider their private feelings in honestly answering the following questions.

The answers are only important for you as part of a larger healing process, not for anyone else.

* In considering the crime of murder, how effectively do you think capital punishment has worked as a deterrent to prevent murder over the past two millenniums or more?
* Does history really give us any hope for the cycle of individual violence and our collective acts of war to end anytime soon?
* Do we have any ideas, suggestions, or plans to help prevent our endless litany of wars?
* Do we first produce war then fear, or is our fear an innate condition that creates the atmosphere of our tragically violent track record? Classic chicken or the egg?
* Where did fear first begin? For mankind? For you?
* Regardless of the origins of fear, is there an antidote for fear, or are we condemned to always be in fear of fear itself?

Whatever you're most private answers may be, one can appreciate the obvious conundrum that these age-old considerations continue to present to all of us.

Now let us examine two conflicting and long-held foundations of religion related to this topic.

1. An all-loving deity created the universe and everything existing within it, including you in "the image and likeness of God."
2. An angry God condemns humans he/she created to hell as unworthy (eternally condemned for their unforgivable offenses).

In considering whether an omnipotent, perfect, and all-loving "God" (Father?) who created us as eternal beings in his/her image (male/female) and loves us unconditionally, then *how in God's name* could we ever be condemned to everlasting punishment in hell by the same loving God?

This reference to gender could take an entire book to address adequately, but for now, suffice to say that in my mind, this patriarchal model has seriously injured a divine balance in our relationship to the sacred feminine and masculine in many ways. To this day, I remain in absolute awe at having received the gift of life from the sacred womb of womanhood. With respect, we owe it to everyone to pursue healing this patriarchal condition that obviously suppresses and shortchanges women while subtly injuring a healthy and secure manhood in tragic ways. Establishing a respectful gender balance invites us to enjoy expanded freedoms born out of a spirit of forgiveness and a most holy "oneness".

I will return later to the relationship between forgiveness and our personal freedoms, but first, we need to more fully understand the nature of punishment. I'd initially ask you to consider if as a mom or dad, you would ever be in such total anger with your child as to decide to disown and condemn them into a state of everlasting suffering. If you struggle to embrace this image of permanently punishing our own children, then is it not inconceivable to think of God placing them or us into an eternal hell?

My honest personal answer is that I, for one, would not cast the first stone, let alone cast away my own child or any other person even if I perceived them in some adversarial role. (The truth is this adversarial perception would itself be flawed since we are all created from the same source, and we could never truly be enemies or be separated from each other as members of the human family.) No matter how pronounced our differences may be, no distinction exist that removes us from being a member of the human race! A more humorous view might be to say that I guess we are all stuck with each other in that "we cannot choose our relatives."

So has this fear of hell been fostered as some misguided deterrent to prevent crimes, killings, and eternal damnation? (As portrayed for example by scriptural scrolls or stone tablets of God's commandments such as "Thou shall not kill.") How effective do you feel this concept has worked? Has it been an effective deterrent to criminal behavior in relating to our various societies or in our religious lives? Haven't all countries in effect legalized killing (to the point of even promoting the glorification of war) while our religious institutions have similarly found a way to accept this paradigm and bless these sacrificial mass killings? To use a current cliché, we have established war over time as the "new normal."

History shows that the powers at hand could establish convenient exceptions to morally justify killing (legally in the name of duty), using such guises as enemies of the state or "evil infidels" who were on a path to hell. This is but one example of societal authorities permitting the righteous killing of "our enemies." Of course, the enemy could be spared if they would submit and comply with our particular views. In reluctant acceptance of our sanctimonious terms, we might then benevolently grant *forgiveness* for their wrongdoings (as in Germany's WWI surrender where punitive reparations were imposed to pay for the tragic destruction inflicted upon both sides). Historians agree that such punitive actions ultimately sowed the seeds of World War II, and germinate they did. If one looks back over the centuries, they can see that times of peace have arguably served as periods of preparation for the next war as our modern-day military-industrial complex marches on as an economic machine that President Dwight Eisenhower once cautioned against. Accepting this convoluted logic only reinforces these cynically destructive cycles, as portrayed in modern Orwellian-like prophecies.

We can also look back and witness how yesterday's vilified enemies can become new economic friends in the years that follow any military conquests (USA, Japan, and Germany). Yet round and round it goes, an insane pattern largely accepted as unavoidable if not even normal. To me it neither seems spiritual nor even productive under any system of values, democratic, despot, or divine. Above all, it is categorically illogical and abnormal. I am not proposing naive pacifism, but I am seeking to gain perspective and better understand the realities we have created to date. Let us clearly see the results we continue to produce. Must we condemn our children to this fate? How we choose to answer questions around punishment and its purposed outcomes is a responsibility belonging to each of us.

- Does compliance with our current codes of justice yield the results we intended or desire?
- Is there not a better way than fear and punishment for establishing a basis for social order?
- How might we better foster respectful relationships, be it individual, institutional, or governmental?

Interestingly enough (like much of our human paradox), no one is solely right or exclusively wrong when it comes to an opinion on war, crime, punishment, rehabilitation, pardoning, or forgiveness. Whether the issue is large or small, between individuals or societies, each viewpoint contains an important observation for us to *understand* and consider in everyone's needs for healing. For instance consider, the following.

❖ The earnest act of a person asking for our pardon with genuine *remorse* for some offense usually strikes a meaningful chord for most human beings to forgive another as a desirable outcome. It also reminds us of those religious texts referring to forgiving, perhaps no more famous than Jesus's biblical command to *forgive* "not once, not seven times, but seven times seventy!" (Is not the implied moral of this story an infinite disposition for forgiveness?)

❖ Christianity's crucifixion account went to the trouble of documenting Jesus *forgiving* the accused criminal next to him, proclaiming he would be with him in heaven that *very day.*

❖ Also chronicled was Christ referencing his own murderers by proclaiming to "*forgive* them, for they know not what they do."

❖ Is it not then conceivable that in our collective ignorance, we have all followed our religious and political leaders (perhaps ignoring our own heart's wisdom) down deadly paths that do not benefit humanity? Perhaps our societies and we, as citizens, remain in the dark and also "do not know what we are doing." We need to awaken from our slumber and give fresh thought to what we are doing now.

So how do we awaken to reconcile these age-old justifications that dismiss us from our responsibility for using the powerful internal potential that we all possess to stop our destructive choices this day? If one accepts premises that all beings are created equally (with the spirit of God residing within each of us), that same spirit begs the question:

For heaven's sake, why do we wait to make changes in the light of new understandings?

Martin Luther King Jr. provided us with a powerful understanding about love and hate when he said, "I have decided to stick with love, as hate is too great a burden to bear."

What would happen if, for just one moment, we could even theoretically release our old understandings that hell even exists? Just pretend as if it is a game at first, meditate for a few days, and then listen once to the lyrics of

John Lennon's famous song titled "Imagine." How would this paradigm change us? How might it change our world?

In a similar chord, I exhort everyone to imagine this as an exercise to consider being back in harmony with God this very day and be forgiven for not fully grasping what we have previously been doing to each other. We could only envision this premise that not one of us will ever be cast to hell but are forever destined to be in the paradise for which we were created. We can choose to accept each other now, or later. Whenever we tire of war and suffering, we can reawaken and realize that we are all prodigal children and are free to return upon a road that leads us to our birthright and homecoming. The good news of this chapter is that it is merely invitation to privately think and begin answering these questions for yourself, as soon as you are ready.

May these poems assist your reflections relative to forgiveness and healing and how it might enhance our individual freedoms for a potentially more peaceful future together.

"Forgiveness is the key to happiness." (*A Course in Miracles*)

Blessed by Balance #1
We are given forgiveness, without any needs,
To submit to dogma, or align with many creeds.

A gift of the Goddess, God's lineage to beings of bliss,
A birthright of the universe, is impossible to miss.

On this balanced scale, equally divine in heaven's sight,
Where together Men and Women both reach the greatest heights,
Within the image of a Goddess, births God's greatest delight.

Artwork by Jimi Tutko

This Moment of Future History

Sorrowful centuries of historical repetitions,
An indictment of man's ADAM-ant convictions.
Repeated through the ages, a pathological path,
Replete with the rages of our illogical wrath.

Strictly adhering to dogma, has it ever struck you?
Our dedication replicates the tried and untrue.
As an EVE-ning breath cleanses, exhaling our fear,
Quenching our thirsty spirits, loving solutions appear.

Theological volumes no longer lead us astray,
Millenniums of madness cease replication today.
We can create a new future as this nation once did,
A Declaration of Independence was also once forbid.

Departures from the past are better understood,
Gazing back upon history from where we once stood.
Envisioning our future destiny, declare it forevermore,
Creating our children's vision of a world without war.
Divesting old ideas, invests in our forgiving convictions,
Resolving our conflicts, absolving historical repetitions.

Richard Francis Moore

Full Circle

Round and round the killing will go,
Cycles of hatred we've all come to know.
Coming full circle, the enemies face did show,
As we viewed ourselves, orbiting our inferno.

Religions faithful soldiers, onward they go,
Deflating our globe, with an inflated ego.
Self-defeating, buried in cemeteries we own,
Life so limited, covered with grass overgrown.

How to stop this ceaseless blaming and blaming,
A cease fire for hatred, still flaming and flaming.
Such grave acts incinerate an inheritance to bestow,
Condemning each generation to a familiar death row.

Such are the seasons, when choosing brevity as life,
Might this prove reason, inspiring peace over strife?
With bombs bursting in air, we blind our sight,
Of more glorious stars beaming heavenly insight.

In the sacred rotation of brother sun, and sister moon,
Revolving spheres shine upon us to light our way soon.
Under new spheres of influence, we envision new creations,
Of a well-rounded human family for future generations.

In breaking this cycle encircled by hate,
A revolution to forgive, let us not hesitate,
Applying the brakes from fostering fear,
Embracing as brothers and sisters so dear.

A genesis of choice awaits the whole human race,
A universal desire, circumventing time and space.
Choosing to rejoice, not going backward in disgrace,
Observing our communion, growing forward in grace.

In the seasons of life, we spin each cycle in turn,
By simply loving one another, we discover and discern.
Salvation is in our hands, the fruits of a forgiving miracle,
In original innocence, our birthright of paradise full circle.

Patriarchy Passing

Permeating the planet,
A powerful pestilence,
The false pride of Presidents,
Premiers, and prime ministers,
Primarily ministering to those in power.
Popes and prelates also administer,
As priests and pastors suppress our sister,
Spewing sinister falsehoods prevents her flower,
Protects a patriarchy in their impenetrable tower.
Observing this old macho man stance,
Reveals an unnatural solo dance,
Devoid of beauty and feminine balance.
Thus the patronizing fall from grace,
An apostasy to all, a humbling disgrace.

Preaching to all prelates, parsons, a papacy and more,
To honor the God and Goddess, our original harmony to restore.
Created in this union, forever from this love,
Remember our reunion, ordained eternally above.
Male reconstruction of men's powerful theology,
False pretense of an angry God, awaits an apology.
Self-destruction denies a loving God throughout history,
Reformation begs deliverance from our recurring misery.

This is true of the world's many religions,
Well intended though they may have been,
Forfeiting the feminine divine for male legions,
Prostituting our goddess for the sake of men.
We may at last end this futile path of death,
Renewing hearts with our loving breath.
Our Pardon will restore paradise to fruition,
As simple forgiveness, ends fruitless repetition.

In the beautiful balance of both yin and yang,
Men and women are thus freed from past pain.
As we break with this past, each shackle and chain,
As sacred creations, we sing our holy refrain;
A heavenly inheritance, bestowed in the creator's name.

Richard Francis Moore

As a patriarchy passes, entering maternal solutions,
Our divine destiny of love, births balanced resolutions.
Love penetrates the discord of any further outrage,
In one accord we will release, the wars that we wage.
Sweet chords diffuse anger with a loving tone,
With free will and forgiveness we thus atone,
Embracing all humankind, were no longer alone.

On that Present Day

Judgment Day
As our prison population continually grows,
Longer lines form, calling for increased rows.
Talking tough terms across our nation,
Double crossed codes create more condemnation,
Judgments will enlarge a national incarceration.

Speaking in prolonged sentences,
Quoting *Bleak House* utterances,
Further shackling the keys to all forgiveness,
Compounded by our criminal defensiveness.

With prisons constructed at an enterprising pace,
We continue to bar, what we dare not face.
In persecuting offenses, we condemn crimes of hate,
But can we also confess we share a common fate?

Disappearing Day
No more fostering of those fearful ways,
A ceasing of rumors and hurtful hearsay,
No longer projecting a fateful doomsday,
Forgiveness paves a road to paradise today.

Like awakening from a nightmare,
Restoring our present without a care
Upon our dreams shedding new light,
The sunrise reveals spiritual insight.

Exposing illusions, we can see so clear,
Our divine natures, our union is so near.

160

With enlightened vision, we light the way,
In our loving truth, hate disappears today.

No more mourning of our tragic play,
Arise this morning, live in awareness we say,
No longer lamenting heavens delay,
By forgiving, our fears disappear today.
A blessing engenders man and woman as divine,
Granting us a godly peace so deep and sublime.

I close this chapter by anonymously quoting a former politician I recently heard addressing university students. Because of the current state of political polarization and paralysis, I intentionally chose to not reveal his name so as not to risk missing the message. His key point while speaking at this nonpolitical forum was to espouse the importance of *balance* in best serving the public interests. He explained that this principle "had often perplexed his own party leadership, and also confused his opposition." He insisted that balance was the same reason that persons considered at least listening to him in private, since he would often cooperate with any program or proposal that he understood would help the greater public in a progressive manner. His track record proved this to be true, regardless of which political party was sponsoring the legislation. His main point, however, was not about boasting about his bipartisan capabilities, but he was making a point that "strict party loyalty is a dangerous tendency when it replaces the basic focus of serving the public good." He spoke further on "this importance of balance in the body politic, and avoiding polarizing rhetoric which can prove harmful to all." The following political poem attempts to addresses this important theme that coincidentally relates to the many perspectives and considerations contained in this book of healing.

"A Cautious Dose of Conservatism and a Light Dose of Liberalism""

I never met a liberal without a sense of social justice,
Whose motivation was nothing less than to benefit our entire society.
I have also never met an extremely liberal ideologue,
That was not bordering on loony, like a dangerous lunar tide,
Drifting further away from the mainland with every stride.

I never met a conservative without concern for the public good,
Of preserving practices that have served society well.
I also have never met an extremely committed conservative,
Fanatically fermenting fear, became crazier than a cuckoo's nest,
Flying further away from the mainland, committed to unrest.

I pray that the Coast Guard on east and west shores,
can navigate all sides back to safer harbors,
Harboring a diverse vision of freedom for all,
A multi colored homeland, reunited we stand tall.

*"God grant that not only the love of liberty but a thorough knowledge
of the rights of man may pervade all the nations of the earth, so that a
philosopher may set his foot anywhere on its surface and say, 'This is my
country.'"*
—Benjamin Franklin

.

Reflections for Healing
(Your Optional Journal)

Chapter 8
Healing
Understanding Forgiveness and Freedom

Did any particular observations catch your attention in this chapter in relation to
   a. forgiveness?

   b. freedom?

Can you think of any instances where you act(s) of forgiveness benefited you and/or others?

Can you see any new paradigms forming to change our world relation to this chapters themes?

Did any poetic mediation prove insightful or helpful in any way?

Your Other Notes:

Chapter 9

Rhythms of Rumi and Songs of Solomon for the New Millennium

Understanding Sexuality and Healing

> *"Sex and spirituality are one and the same—we are all born through sex, and hence it is through sex that we can connect back to our spirit."*
> *—Lao Tzu*

Beginning with this perspective of Lao Tzu's ancient counsel, I endeavor to address our sexuality from a highly positive and productive new light. Our world history has more often portrayed our naturally loving expression of sexuality in negatively framed undertones. Well intended or not, these characterizations of limited or even forbidden fruits tend to quietly and unnaturally suppress what should be a norm and a naturally proud expression of affection to our beloved ones. Suppression of any genuine human feelings often yields harmful results as pressures rise to the surface over time.

In my life, I have witnessed that when sexual expression has no healthy outlet for whatever reasons, various forms of abuse and exploitation can be manifested. Negative results may appear merely as a subtly silent muting of this glorious loving gift of creation, or may be demonstrated in a more harmful manner by overtly misusing the mystical miracle of our capacity for sexual union. At this point in human history, a new millennium presents us a unique opportunity to review and discuss engendering a more positive and beneficial view of our sexuality. With fresh perspective, we might effectively readdress, reframe, and renew our loving sexual relationships in a profoundly divine way—profound in terms of a simplicity that lovingly supports the beautiful bliss intended for both body and spirit since our creation. It is a taste of paradise and our common union that bore us all and is thus our birthright to celebrate.

With the stated intention of acknowledging our human sexuality as a blessing and a gift of mystical unity, we can positively recognize the joyful manner in which we are all gloriously and eternally connected. This perspective is generally in contrast to many negative historical treatments of

sexuality that inferred sex was somehow an inherently ungodly path or, at
the very least, a distraction from the divine. Yet the reality of living a healthy
sexual life offers us the potential of experiencing abundant love as we more
fully explore and express our intimacy with our beloved. Yes, the acts of
human love provides us with an important glimpse into comprehending the
link to our universal bond. A mystifying glory can be found when we share
such physical, emotional, and spiritual oneness, revealing a deep sense of
our dual nature as physical and eternal beings. Let us view this topic anew
from east to west, joining in spirit with the ancient wisdom spoken by King
Solomon and later Rumi to write a new chapter in humanities unfolding love
story waiting to fully flower.

"Let him kiss me with the kisses of his mouth: for thy love is better than
wine" (Song of Solomon, 1:2).

This chapter will conclude Act II which emphasizes an understanding
of the *present* in relation to our healthy *interdependence* upon each other.
Our sexuality presents us with a dynamic and obvious demonstration of
our interdependence upon each other and, at the same time, supports our
healthy independence, inasmuch as real love does not own or possess but
endeavors to support our growth and liberate our spirits in ecstatic ways.

Continuing with our overarching theme to better understand the
healing power within each of us, it is essential we consider the paradigms
that have surrounded our human sexuality to this moment. Only then can
we move forward to Act III and address a healthier future. In this effort, I
will attempt to interweave various facets of this broad subject and hopefully
help us see the big picture that invites us to utilize our sensuality to support
and heal one another. I end the introduction of this chapter by asking a
question.

**Why do you think the topic of our human sexuality is often an
uncomfortable subject for discussion?**

In reading this chapter about the wonderful dimension of our sensual
nature, I encourage all too playfully visualize being cuddled up in a
comforting quilt to enjoy this as a sort of inspiring adult bedtime story.

One such inspiration was a historically significant experience that
occurred as I turned eighteen years of age. The relevance of these unusual
circumstances is the imprint left upon me in the form of my lifelong
wonderment and appreciation in the inherent beauty to be found in our
sexuality. In my youthful innocence, I was exposed to extraordinary sights

and scenes that provided a healthy impetus for me to reevaluate the rigid (albeit well intended) concepts of sexuality with which I was raised.

Back in 1969, I had just completed my junior year in high school, one that tragically concluded with the death of my father. As I turned eighteen, I quickly secured two jobs over the summer to assist our family in difficult circumstances. As summer went on, my appreciative mother lovingly suggested that I take time to do something fun before returning for my senior year in school. In brief I had spoken with three friends about going camping at an outdoor concert being advertised on the radio in the Catskill Mountains. With my mother's blessing, we convinced my brother to give us a ride on his way to New York City. Unbeknownst to almost everyone, this concert in the country was spontaneously growing into a social gathering that exceeded any planned expectations. It would subsequently catch the world's attention in what became known as Woodstock. While the parade of iconic musicians was the primary captivation, they would become secondary to the many impressions this experience had upon me.

There I spent three extraordinarily peaceful days with approximately 500,000 young people who gathered with civility and a genuine sense of community. This was in stark contrast to a decade of national upheaval, strained by unending war protests, race riots, and political assassinations. A conscious spirit of helpfulness grew as the crowds swelled as did our collective awareness that we were all sharing in some uncharted territory and uncertain outcome of this expression of the human spirit. The mutual support and cooperation of nearly half a million strangers was extraordinary, as if everyone knew we were all in fact individually responsible for creating a positive environment together.

This was despite a growing realization that our physical circumstances were becoming increasingly refugee-like with a lack of any real authority, inadequate food, water, sanitary facilities, or phone booths to communicate with the outside world. Personally, this was no small concern as the ability of my brother to rendezvous and drive us home in three days was against the odds as most outside routes were now closed off by the police and National Guard. Living in an accidental city that lacked infrastructure and services, it was amazing we felt safe with no evident crime or aggressive competition. I experienced people openly sharing their limited resources of food, drink, and shelter along with offering a helping hand. There was certainly behavioral imperfections to be seen, but the prevailing atmosphere remained overwhelmingly positive throughout wind, rain, mud, and, of course, great music almost 24–7.

The related purpose for this background is to place you in an atmosphere that was marked by a good deal of public nudity. It is never easy to describe oneself as naive, but after twelve years of a strict Catholic education, I now found myself in a polar opposite world. My uncomfortable modesty slowly calmed amid so many displays of affection all around me. I was ill at ease, but I was struck by the respectful gentleness offered to each other, and I never witnessed any displays of vulgarity. What I witnessed was both physical and emotional beauty. There were no orgies, but I did see loving displays I'd describe more as Eden-like celebrations.

One tangible example was on a hot afternoon, I hiked over to nearby White Lake for a refreshing swim. Arriving at the shoreline, I was both frightened and delighted to find hundreds of people, mostly skinny dipping. As I timidly put my big toe in the water, the natural beauty of youth was obvious, but what really surprised me was the pervading feeling of joy and safety, not finding a place of arousal but a happy one for sure. After my initial hesitation, I came to enjoy the water as well as the refreshing conversation among people naturally being in each other's presence. Despite the powerful hormonal influences of youth, I never did observe any unwanted intrusion upon a person's private space. Admittedly, I was internally conflicted by my own cultural-religious background (one in which sex was rarely ever spoken of), but I was also in a very happy and peaceful place.

I entered and left Woodstock with my youthful innocence but my exposure to so many beautiful expressions of our sexuality assured me that my natural feelings should not be repressed but valued, so long as my intentions remained genuine and loving. To this day, I remain feeling privileged to have participated in this beautifully blessed and peaceful assembly.

Can this experience tell us anything about ourselves in terms of sexuality and healing? As always, only your answers are important!

I am not suggesting this vignette on Woodstock is the answer to any sexual dysfunctions, nor am I recommending that we seek out a half million friends to go camping with in all of our glory. My purpose in citing this one-time phenomenon is because it provided an accidental and powerful social laboratory that just might offer some insights for a more positive understanding of our sexuality in beautifully balanced ways. For instance, as just one of hundreds of thousands of individuals who unexpectedly found themselves placed in an extremely opposite social environment, I took pause to reflect upon these circumstances. I recall thinking that on the previous Sunday, I took my siblings to our ritual attending of Catholic mass. One week later, I watched the sunrise as I lay surrounded by couples cuddled in their sleeping bags while enjoying the sounds of "The Who" completing a three-hour performance. I also thought of some friends and other parishioners who I knew at this same moment were serving in the war torn conditions of Vietnam. Such extreme experiences usually have lessons to teach us in any given area of our lives, be it diet, drinking, working, playing, or sex. As usual, everyone is impacted differently by any event, and I benefited by seeing so many tender moments in stark contrast to the prevailing violence overseas and displayed daily throughout my nation at that time.

My intuition continues to believe that various aspects of healing are linked to having a better understanding of our sexuality in balanced and positive ways—ways that transcend the limiting legal, political, financial, cultural, and religious understandings of gender and sexuality to date. Take a moment and consider this relationship before we view life through other prisms. What do you think?

Continuing to probe the topic we will now take time to consider our sexuality as a naturally beautiful, healthy, and noble expression. Here we might better comprehend our miraculous design within includes those DNA bonds implanted in our being in a manner that can assist our healing and spirituality. As an undeniably essential aspect of our existence, sexual energy can possesses a powerful source for human healing. Failure to include this topic in relation to healing risks leaving open old wounds that still fester within humanity from longstanding seeds once sown that produced negative paradigms marked by repression and control. At this time in human history, I believe it is critically important that we come to recognize the positive healing energy contained within this powerful gift of creation and procreation. Our future ability to more openly engage each other in intimate sexual relationship is an awesome privilege that should be encouraged within a healthy balance marked by a genuine authenticity. Such a place exists in the human heart in between the extremes of fearful repression and reckless license. The healthy balance of gender in relation to mutual respect and appreciation for each other will also require further reflection.

The exquisite energetic of human sexuality is not only a powerful individual experience; it is also an obvious bonding experience between partners that can demonstrate for us a symbolic spiritual unity with our fellow beings. (Note with a smile that even atheists and agnostics have been known to innately vocalize a passionate "oh my god" at the moment of orgasm.) This understanding can provide us with an insightful and beautiful healing human experience. In this context of sexual union between individuals, imagine if you will this being a small preview of the collective awe to be experienced when an eternally created race of human beings inevitably reunite with our original source. Whether we believe in scientific theories, religious traditions, or both, we will inevitably leave our transient earthly physical bodies, and our energy will return to its source.

Hsi Lai writes, "If you cannot face directly your sexuality, you will never discover your true spirituality" (Hsi Lai transcriptions of three-thousand-year-old Taoist masters' teachings from the *White Tigress Manual*).

The Dalai Lama once advised that "one can live without religion, or even without meditation, but we cannot survive without human touch." During my fifteen years of professionally supporting the work of nurses, they often used the term "healing touch" in relation to contributing to their recovering patients. While this term *touch* was used in a clinical sense and not as a sexual reference, it did make me think. If a simple reassuring physical touch from a nurse to a patient possesses a healing impact, then how much more powerful must the tender touch be between loved ones? Eventually, I had the privilege of speaking with world renowned sex researchers (two former deans from the SUNY at Buffalo), Dr. Bonnie and Dr. Vern Bullough, who sadly are both now deceased.

In my visits with Vern over the years at his California home, our discussions led him to present me with a copy of his book *Science in the Bedroom (A History of Sex Research)*. I found it insightful especially in terms of information on human sexuality that is rarely discussed and often misunderstood. Like Dr. Bullough's book, I want to clarify with a quick disclaimer that I am not addressing this subject in the context of moral, legal, cultural mores, or religious dogma. All these may have their place, but I am simply addressing how healing and sexuality are potentially enjoined in incredibly positive ways that can further benefit our overall well-being. One might see this as rather obvious, but I believe it is beneficial to more fully address it.

So why does examining our sexuality often trigger sensitivities that can make us uncomfortable? Here are just a few personal observations and insights I have identified. (You may have others.)

1. On one hand, we all seem more conditioned to the norms of popular literature that regularly provides awards, accolades, and honors to authors who capture many aspects of the violent expressions of the human experience. From graphic portrayals of our chronic wars, criminal behavior, and other fearful dysfunctions, our culture does not really flinch at books, movies, or television series graphically depicting these violent realities. On the other hand, the open sharing of information exploring our sexuality and our passionate sexual experiences remains a largely uncomfortable conversation for the general population. In reality, serious

conversations about celebrating our sexuality are often a subject not well received in public or in polite company. Why is that?

2. To further clarify, I am *not* referring here to the irony of easily available bawdy television shows, seductive sexual cinema, or Internet pornography. (Oddly such television is often viewed as socially acceptable and treated as sexually liberated conversation at the office cooler or lunchroom.) As indicated, I am not suggesting some new restrictive moral code, but I am endeavoring to advance a more open, comfortable, and elevated level of communicating our beautifully sacred and sensual dimensions. *Informed and intelligent conversation can be a healing balm.* So can we create a more balanced atmosphere to better demonstrate our natural affection for each other as adults? If so, can we find ways to positively address raising our children with honest information that provides them with a healthy understanding of their emerging sexuality? Positive discussions could prove helpful to young and old alike.

3. While emphasizing the positive, it is unfortunately impossible to address sexuality with integrity unless we honestly recognize the many destructive and dysfunctional realities that have harmfully violated so many individuals. As predatory sexual offenses continue to plague humankind, we cannot ignore discussing this dark and exploitive side of sexuality. Let's acknowledge some more universal examples of flagrantly negative expressions of our sexuality, like child abuse, rape, sexual slavery, forced prostitution, and even abuses within a marriage, to cite a few. While our purpose does not focus in depth on any singular concern, we cannot fail to comprehend the harmful pains inflicted on victims by their predators. It is worth knowing that these very predators are often repeating an abusive cycle emerging from their own painful experience. Like all excesses, the burning question is how to break the cycle? Building awareness is at least one step to begin healing.

Like electricity, our powerful sexual energy can be used for our great benefit, or it can result in destructive injury. While I am personally fortunate not to have been scarred by any extreme offenses, I have unfortunately known men and woman who have suffered various traumatic forms of sexual violations, ranging from exploitive scout leaders to pedophile priests abusing youngsters to women who have been both beaten and raped. I am happy to report that in speaking to these dear individuals as adults, they had received much loving support and counsel in courageously facing their past traumas and eventually move into a place of healing.

I have chosen to cite such hurtful sexual transgressions in order to explore some possible reasons (*not* justifications) for what prompts such tragic behaviors ever being committed in the first place. As I have already inferred I believe at least one connection might partially stem from our world's repression of our sexuality. Simply stated, I have observed that systematic repression of any aspect of life (be it social, cultural, or religious, etc.) can build up a pressure that is certain to express itself and explode elsewhere. Suppressed feelings often resurface and are later released in damaging ways! As addressed in chapter 8, despite very good intentions, the familiar concept of "forbidden fruit" has arguably never proved very effective in altering antisocial behaviors such as murder, theft, or sexual transgressions.

In contrast, it is my belief that by discussing our sexuality in a more positive framework, it may help us see a relationship between our spiritual dimension and our sexual expressions. I am posing the possibility that establishing an intentionally sex positive outlook and a more open dialogue with each other (including our children) could go a long way toward reducing abuses of all sorts by establishing a more loving and unified world. Such a frame of reference would encourage us to approach sex as a path to the divine, and consequently reduce the false feelings of separation from each other and creation/creator. Separation and isolation produce fearful outcomes as is so destructively documented throughout human history to date. If you think that a lack of love and ongoing wars are not coincidentally linked, I suggest you give it further thought.

I thus encourage further consideration as to how the negative sexual behaviors we abhor may in part be a by-product of our resistance to openly discuss and express our positive sexuality. The unspoken messages of our silence, abstinence, and denial (while not necessarily harmful in itself) can over time serve to create unintended but oppressive social codes that can grow like a cancer within, stifling our own loving growth and emerge as harmful exploitations of the innocent. Simply stated, when human beings struggle to find socially acceptable sexual expressions, the suppressed feelings will find a way to boil over with a destructive force, similar to that of an overheated nuclear reactor. We need to gift humanity by positively blessing sexuality!

I also contend that we can use our sensual nature to directly provide us with an integral link to our own power for human healing through our blessed sexuality! Science can also attest to certain physical benefits of sex beginning with the releasing of endorphins as but one example. My assertions of healing are based more upon my personal experiences in communicating with others during the course of life. Many positive behaviors can be observed in the afterglow of sexual love such as increased emotional joy, closeness to loved ones, a calm and restful peace, and a greater willingness to more compassionately assist our fellow beings, to cite just a few.

4. Another reason for some discomfort with sexual discussions may lie under the more veiled confusion of our noisy and hectic modern world. Amid this hurried pace has emerged a global culture heavily dominated by technology and scientific advancement, along with an over load of electronic communications. While these influences have a positive side to connect us in sharing information worldwide, they also have another side that can lessen emotional expression and deprive us of time for cultivating deeper inter personal relationships.

5. A final thought regarding our hesitancy for verbal social intercourse on healthy sexuality might be gleaned through the eyes of archeology and anthropology. As various indigenous cultures are unearthed and rediscovered, their histories sometimes reveal their approaches to healing along with ancient social mores and sexual practices. As modern science uncovers many written and oral traditions, old knowledge is resurfacing that may be beneficial for us to explore and consider (not dissimilar to how religion draws upon guidance from old traditions). From matriarch models to religious priestesses and goddess traditions, we are being reintroduced to some past perspectives lost to us over time. With the stresses upon relationships in our world (Such as a divorce rate over 50 percent), do these viewpoints around gender have anything to tell us today? Religion often appeals to the "faith of our fathers" as an anchor to societal values, but should we also be considering the "faith of our mothers" (as we were all birthed from a woman's womb) to try and better relate to each other? Can other historical practices help us work through the confusing and conflicting modern imagery in regard to our sexual identities as presented to us in our modern media? Only we can choose to come to some more positive understandings of our sacred sexuality in its many miraculously diverse forms.

From these initial perspectives, might there be new paradigms on the horizon that could give birth to our new and improved sexual performance as a human race? Let's move on.

Examples of ancient insights on sexuality are found in many different traditions. For the specific purpose of studying our positive sexuality, I have chosen to explore one example as articulated in the ancient teachings of an eastern form of Tantra. I was first introduced to these concepts by a tantric practitioner at a healing seminar in Arizona, and I was intrigued to find Tantra as a surprisingly positive perspective on our sexuality. It piqued my interest instantly. To be sure, I am *not* presenting it as a holy grail or even as a recommendation for anyone to pursue, but it does, however, present us with some unique perspectives, which were new to me.

First, know that Tantra is neither a religion nor a philosophy, yet its practice articulates the purposeful understanding of our sacred sexuality. Additionally, it professes an intention of utilizing our sensual energy for sexual healing in a manner integrated into the whole of human experience, both physically and metaphysically. Let me explain further. A basic assertion of Tantra (in its original Eastern tradition but not so much with Western misunderstandings) affirms our essential spiritual nature in a manner that supports our physical human sexuality by positively linking our human healing to understanding our divinity. This is in stark contrast to sex often being viewed negatively as a distraction from our spiritual path to godliness, as many religions have portrayed intentionally or not.

Beyond viewing sex as an innately holy expression, Tantra also promotes developing a heightened awareness and consciousness helping to attain an evolved enlightenment. Furthermore, Tantra fulfills the spiritual by addressing practical physical knowledge around our mystical male and female natures. By providing a wealth of useful information on human sexuality, this ancient tradition offers our modern world fresh insights at a time when our popular culture still remains in the dark on important yet unspoken sexual information. Despite bookstores offering an abundance of books on a multitude of sexual subjects, the personal computer connecting us to all manner of sexual content, still I was fifty-five years of age when I first stumbled upon the revelations of Tantra and sacred sexuality. Having been married for thirty-one years at that point, I was quite astounded to be absorbing so much new information on sex. I am not referring to some Kama Sutra renderings, but in fact, it was a much deeper integration of physical knowledge within the metaphysical dimensions of our existence. I became only more intrigued, and I happily pass along some worthwhile resources (and perhaps revelations) that I was once privileged to be presented with. Ten years later, these lessons continue to enrich me. If you're interested pursuing this further study, the following books are available in any mall bookstore.

- *Finding God Through Sex by* David Deida. Deida beautifully captures the tantric precept of *sexual sacredness* in this uniquely spiritual book.
- *Tantric Orgasm for Women* by Diana Richardson
- *The Multi-Orgasmic Man* by Mantak Chia and Douglas Abrams
- *The Heart of Tantric Sex by* Diana Richardson. Diana shares how a man and woman can learn how to experience a unrushed and prolonged union that is simultaneously mystical, spiritual, physical, and emotional in what has been described as an out-of-body experience for two.

A reminder that the point of considering past cultural practices is not to convince or sell anyone a particular point of view. The purpose here is to demonstrate that we still have much to learn about our sexuality. By citing an experience that is likely unfamiliar to our own background (like Tantra), it can hopefully provide a frame of reference that helps us better understand our own sensuality from an ancient sacred context. By considering other vantage points, we are open to discover new understandings of life beyond the often limiting views we may have been raised with. Whatever our background may be, there is no need to judge or be critical of our own traditions or upbringing. Our focus here is only to help us increase our awareness by sharing other available information. The choices along your journey are forever up to you to freely consider as to whether or not this information holds any relevance in your life.

Ultimately, our context here is to understand any healing aspects of our sexuality that might benefit us when integrated with our divine and human natures. All of this poses fresh questions to reconsider.

- How much of the perverse sexual preying upon other innocent beings might be greatly reduced if only our cultures, religions, and world would courageously communicate more openly about our sexuality? A greater appreciation of our healthy needs and desires could prove beneficial.

- Can framing the topic of sex as the Creator's positive intention for us to express our divine sexual bliss make it more acceptable? If so, would this be the start of a healthier open discussion of sex for both religious and secular institutions?

A greater collective understanding of our healthy sexuality, has the potential to provide us a much more positive paradigm for the future of love and the functioning of our world.

Once again, I conclude this chapter with meditative poetry that conveys an important aspect of our ability to come together to touch each other and heal each other in a most powerful and profound manner! In the essential spirit of past written traditions such as the biblical book the Song of Solomon and the poetry of Rumi, I hope you will understand the beautiful intentions expressed in the following poetry.

These verses were an inspired attempt to express the inexpressible beauty we possess to fully celebrate loving each other in the most intimate of holy human embraces. I end with a remembrance to fully embrace the human family as part of one creation by recalling another biblical exhortation: "to love one another as ourselves."

Touching the World

To change the world,
We must touch the heart of the matter,
What matters most to our human hearts?
Both men and women must do their part,
With tender touch, a new paradigm to impart,
As feminine balance engenders a promising fresh start.

In this our awaited promised land,
A woman's love is so miraculous to understand.
A woman's glance, gladdens the heart,
Her tender touch awakens body and soul.
Her caresses were created, for the body to know.

Her kiss can rekindle our muted spirits,
With kind words she reshapes emotions,
In kind we recall true feminine devotions.
Such is her innate and divine presence,
A state of goodness, her loving essence.

Just as women have brought forth men to be,
Born out of this new balance, we are further set free.
Our entire environment is altered by her loving word,
Our touch can recreate a powerfully healed world.

Whether you are young or old, male or female, single, married, or celibate, human touch is an important aspect of everyone's life. Heartfelt human touch can help heal our individual needs before rippling outward into our greater world. As I often reminded my children, our world's biggest problem does not emanate from too many people loving each other with care and joy, but why in God's name are so many people killing one another in hatred?

The next four poems are grouped together for the dedicated expression of honoring and respecting femininity as a divine gift of love for all seasons. While I unapologetically write from a male perspective endeavoring to express my heartfelt adoration to honor the Goddess in every woman, I am equally honoring the divine essence of God implanted in each man. The reason for this is to directly address our reverence for the natural balance between genders and our deep seeded desire for committed loving relationships in their many forms. These poems seek to offer inspiration and insight as to why this has been such a great source of disappointment and frustration to men and women for millenniums.

"I would love to kiss you! When soul rises, into lips, you feel the kiss you've wanted" (Rumi).

"A Love for All Seasons"

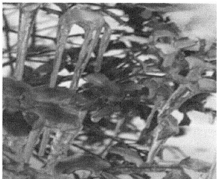

Photo by Richard F. Moore

1. Within Women Warms a Winter Solstice

W   Women Wear Within, Wisdom's Womb,

I   Internally Inspired, Intuition Is Infused,

N   Necessarily Nurturing Nucleus Needs.

T   Two Terrestrials Tenderly Touch Temples,

E   Ecstatically Emitting Embryonic Energy,

R   Rotating Revolutions, Render Restful Renewal.

<u>S</u>   Sacred Sexuality, Sensing Symbiotic Satisfaction,

<u>O</u>   Our Omnipresent Oneness, Oscillating Overhead.

<u>L</u>   Lavishly Loving, Lushly Layered Latitudes,

<u>S</u>   Supreme Sequences, Sowing Spiritual Seasons,

<u>T</u>   Timed Testimony, Toward Timeless Truth,

<u>I</u>   Incarnating Into Insightful Intelligence.

<u>C</u>   Constant Co-Creation, Caresses Caring Cocoons,

<u>E</u>   Effervescent Emanations, Empirically Eternal.

Winter Solstice sunset
Photo by Richard F Moore
It is often in the darkest of days, where true light is best observed.

2. Springtime Streams of Love

Photo by Richard F. Moore

Richard Francis Moore

Amid spring rains so softly streaming.
Loving rays of light leave me beaming,
Illuminating my soul with this sunny shower,
A rainbow of warmth from a blooming flower.
Rites of spring emerge in stream and field,
Observing new life, our senses thus yield.
A cycle displays nature's beautiful power,
A mystical spray rains from a heavenly tower.

The sun shines upon the face of creation,
As birds and bees busy with pollination
Pheromones Spring forth in waves of radiance,
Nature nurtures a most fragrant essence.
All life abounds with playful celebration,
To spring time joys, they join in participation.
These waters of life will sustain procreation,
A Refreshing love flows, in universal relation.

Wet from these rains, drenched in this light,
Appreciating the beauty, of this unfolding sight.
Sharing such warmth, distills fear and fright,
Restoring the soul's roots with original insight.
A golden sun, showers earthly places,
As droplets of spring, bless personal spaces.
Bathed in this warm and loving glow,
As souls are restored, hearts can grow.

I breathe in deeply my flowers sweet scent,
Both body and spirit empower my ascent.
Moisture sustains the growth of sacred seed,
Cleansed by this love our natures so need,
Rekindling our first holy remembrance.
Remembering to love all without hindrance.

From xylem to phloem, Loving streams make total sense,
Absorbing each other, merging rebirths our essence.

3. Immersion in Sacred Spaces

Photo by Richard F Moore

Sheer spirit and pleasure,
Summer's warmth to treasure.
Dark illusions evaporate in loves glow,
Emerging from a mist, arises a rainbow.

In such sacred spaces, true colors show
Outward my energies openly flow,
I am frozen in her sunny heat,
My heart melts in willing defeat.

A surrendering of my will,
So willingly occupied,
Spellbound I am still,
Within mother earth preoccupied.

A powerful sharing so freely falls,
Refreshing us from its watery walls
Deepening breaths, cleansing strife,
Watery depths, produce exotic life.

Submerged in our most primal mooring,
Enraptured, entwined, embraced,
Until the light of a new morning,
Within a woman's presence, my being is graced.

The feminine divine, a soul's revelation,
Her restoring touch could save every nation.
Our world needs a woman's good graces,
Submitting to her holy and sacred spaces,

The Sacred Feminine, a goddess revealed.
Restoring her place leads us to be healed.
So taste her goodness, breath in her scents,
Healing in our oneness, she is heaven sent.

Sheer pleasure revealed through the mist,
Rainbows lighten hearts, as softly as a kiss.
A Goddess to Treasure, by day or night.
Many blessings to you, in love and light

Photo by Richard F Moore

4. Fallen Fruits and Harvesting Paradise

It is never too late to return to our origin,
And harvest the fruits that wait within.
With hearts overflowing, our spirits are enjoying,
This bountiful reunion, God and Goddess
enjoining.

I caress creations curves so beautifully bending,
Feelings emerge from our every nerve ending.
Throughout our bodies energy is sending,
The tree of life to produce love never ending.

So consuming is this consummation,
Symbolic reunion of every nation,
A communion of every being,
A love beyond what our eyes are seeing,
Past, present, and everyone's future,
Fulfilling our purpose, in union we nurture.

In preparing to open her fertile flower,
She slowly raises this phallic tower,
Subtle scented petals, fresh and moist,
A pause so pregnant, a preface to rejoice.

At the threshold of her holy garden,
Floral incense rises to fully hearten,
In the heartfelt merging, of two into one,
Melts the firmest flesh, this Goddess of sun.
A sacred sexuality, meant to be embraced,
Given this gift, we are forever graced.

Adoration is natural in a garden of pleasure,
Worshiping the creation of our deep treasure,
Paradise provides these fruits for our tasting,
These blessed pursuits produce a heavenly
pulsating.

Waves of pleasure, both given and received,
Blend into a oneness, a miracle conceived.
The tree of knowledge, conceives love & being,
Seeds have grown for our universal seeing.
Sensual gifts grown in the garden of creation,
Reproduce a harvest for a bountiful celebration.

Sensing

Sensing one's touch,
Touching my soul
The power is such,
That all should know
In delightful caressing,
We are enlightened so.

To sense silks touching,
Softness meeting firmness,
Suppleness is life affirming,
Softly greeting life's hardness.

Moistly nourishing our thirsty skin,
Permitting penetration deep within.
Sensually searching for our hearts,
Healing the past, freeing fresh starts.

Such is the solace of sensual touch,
Searing the sadness, healing so much.
Touching and tasting, inhaling the scents,
Sensing our goodness in all its Resplendence.

Such a heat, melds the hardest of flesh,
Forging a lush union, we willingly mesh.
Vigorously enjoining, gently absorbing,
Softly we sense our hearts transforming.

An angel, a friend, spirit and soul,
The power of touch, we all should know
With loving caresses, we are enlightened so,
Healing and guiding us in the afterglow

Passion Births Compassion

Loving Passion births true compassion,
As sexual fusion heals cultural confusion.

Embracing others, unleashes hearts to arise,
Realizing love need not be rationalized,
Giving rise to hugs we no longer ration.

A breathtaking beat, within our heart's space,
A global warming, that benefits the human race.

A holy resonance within, echo's harmonious cores.
Orgasmic waves ripple out, from our personal shores,
Departing from the past, we now open our present,
Of God's loving gift to us, of passionate compassion.

Apathy Penetrated

Can a shot of love penetrate the grief?
Affection is infectious, in providing relief!
Loves gifts are theoretically extolled,
Yet often unused and undiscovered,
Sadly unseen rendering hearts left cold,
In hypocrisy they lie unopened and covered.

In failing to go down below the surface,
Were unable to inhale life's sacred scents,
Nor tasting nectars, due to raising hellish fears,
Cultural codes cover our eyes, silencing ears.

Loving appetites are slowly suppressed,
Heavy spirits sink, so lowly depressed.
Creating a cocoon of acquired apathy,
Lacking love in our sterilized sanctuary.

Recalling your inheritance, hearts realerted,
Your loving nature need not be deserted.
So act to reclaim your just deserts,
Reopening hearts, healing what hurts,
Permitting your passions, love flows,
With renewed hearts, ones cup overflows.

Allowing one self to receive pleasure supreme,
To be absorbed by the love of another being,
Penetration to the soul, transcends gender and time,
Receiving becomes giving, beyond reason or rhyme.

The Gift of Sexual Healing
What a supreme gift,
A power to arouse,
Spirits to uplift,
With only a browse,
A union divinely befit,
In awe we can only espouse.

Why was it ever suppressed?
Why so institutionally controlled?
Leaving many souls stressed,
By culturally coding sex as bad and bold.

In hiding our treasures,
In some dark backroom,
We inhibit our pride,
Beyond groom and bride
Such righteous repressions,
Block our beautiful force,
Unleashing expressions,
Of an unholy source.

Denying natural desire gives birth to perversions,
Fostering illegitimate behaviors and self-justifications.
Religious leaders seduce the powerless to pray,
Exploiting these souls upon whom they prey.

Who cast this light,
Of sexuality forbade,
Bad in whose sight?
If lovingly conveyed.

Who said you were naked?
Such an image of dismay.
Made in God's image,
No need to hide in any way.

The world needs love, to cease glorifying violence,
We need kisses and hugs, not subdued in silence.
Gifts are meant to be open, to liberally love and use,
As our hearts reopen, so shall we end the abuse.

In the Name of Loving
(Illusions Unveiled)

By any name under heaven, blessed will you be,
Mary's feminine form, a sacred inward sanctuary.
By all that is holy, in creations outward infinity,
Within your loving garden, births a blessed creativity.

As a name conveys selected vibrations,
An Inspired breath exhales loving emanations.
Miriam, may you feel the loving presence,
In mutual merging of our spiritual essence.

Thirsting for a *Mayim* well of loving solutions,
A Goddesses insights lift the veil of ill illusions,
Your oasis in sight, droplets refresh from afar,
No mirage as love guides a glowing *Mayan* star.

Within *Magdalene's* sanctuary grows a Godly garden,
Lush with laurel, graced with victory garlands.
Under this rooted tree, I rest and thrive,
From wellsprings loving feelings arrive.

Miryam further enriches a deepening name,
Pleasing both prophetess and mankind the same.
Blessed are you among woman as divinity,
A blessing of forgiveness for all humanity.

No more illusions, as the truth is plain to see,
Eyes and hearts open to creation's community.
The gift of a *goddess*, sense her sanctity,
By *any name* under heaven, *merry* will we be.

"I, you, he, she, we . . .
    . . . In the garden of mystic lovers, these are not true distinctions"
(Rumi).

185

Blessed by Balance II

In securing the blessing of the feminine divine,
I was granted a peace so deep and sublime,
I was given forgiveness, without a need,
To submit to any dogma, or required creed.
A gift from the goddess, blesses men with true bliss,
A birthright of the universe one need not miss.
In renewed balance, divine insights are engendered,
A female sanctuary delivers our birthright as rendered.

Loving More

Passionately, I have thus submitted
That loving more must now be permitted
A resuscitation of the hurting human heart
Equals eradication of that which keeps us apart
Only love exists, only love can restore
Lovingly submitted, enriched forevermore.

The Meaning of Love by Rumi

Both Light and Shadow are the dance of Love,
Love has no cause; it is the astrolabe of God's secrets.
Lover and Loving are inseparable and timeless.

Although I may try to describe Love, when I experience it I am speechless.
Although I may try to write about love I am rendered helpless;
My pen breaks and the paper slips away at the ineffable place,
Where Lover and Loving are one.

Every moment is made glorious by the light of Love.

Photo by Richard F. Moore

Artistic Appreciation
Upon her my eyes softly gaze,
Heavenly forms light us ablaze.
Beckoning with every elegant curve,
Flowing with each sway and swerve.

Drawing my attention to each mystical line,
My hands now trace her to touch the divine.
Lips speak in adoring magical curves,
Drawing together deep-rooted nerves.

See the miracle of our delightful design,
A vision to behold from the fruits of the vine.
Such a blessed feast, a harvest of life,
Taming our beasts, an exorcism of strife.

A playful celebration for all of our senses,
Our mutual merging thus commences.
Essentially a reunion for our souls' fresh start,
An exquisite union as two create one work of art.

A blessing for both, loves scented fragrances,
Further enhance our manifold senses.
Inhaling each breath, our hearts know,
Droplets of love nourish body and soul.

Sensual gifts bestow heavenly energy to heal,
With unclouded vision, we see the sacred appeal.
Exposing our oneness, in God's image and name,
Like clouds and crystals, intimacy is never the same.

In final summary of this chapter, it is hard to ignore our subject of sexuality without addressing the nature of committed relationships. So it is I will conclude by briefly examining the current state of the institution of marriage in modern times. I have personally come to believe that the growing levels of marital stress are at least partially the result of centuries of ingrained patriarchal behaviors. They have arguably produced distorted images that project a sense of ownership and possession, which produces resentments and disrespect right back in the direction of men. Like tectonic plates, this silent friction goes unseen and unheard until the foundation of union is shattered. Yes, this is a grand oversimplification but it does effectively paint a picture of one stress fracture. Whether intended or simply a sub-conscious response, the sad statistics of marriage provide exhibit A in the mounting evidence of eroding marital relationships.

But why? How would you answer some of these questions that lie before us?

With over 50 percent of marriages ending in divorce or separation, what of the remaining numbers?

How many of the remaining marriages (% percent) are marked by some form of infidelity?

How many couples stay together only for mutual security, economic, or other pragmatic forces?

How many couples remain together due to religious or societal constraints?

In a more positive vein, do some remain together because they have found a way to freshly renew and grow in their love?

Perhaps others have discovered how to exercise their free will to express an unconditional gift to love and learn from each other in each unfolding moment?

For fear you suspect that I am trying to debunk the almost universal desire of enjoying the fruits of committed loving relationships, *I am not.* Living happily with my life partner for over forty years, I am suggesting that our longstanding paradigm of marriage as an *institution* may in part be contributing to the disillusionment of our originally cherished and committed relationships. We cannot say "I do" only to wake up after the honeymoon to treat each other as possessions to be owned or act as though that due to religious and legal obligations that one or the other party is now *trapped.* Far too often, these conditioned behaviors are cloaked within an oppressive psychology, but they cannot be hidden from the heart. Our inner wisdom recognizes the subtle body language of any discontent. These unspoken feelings can produce negative emotions that if not addressed pose great risk to our relationships and our future health. I believe it is here where sexuality can foster our health or permit illness to take root by manifesting any number of maladies.

In brief, I exhort all of us to make love with the passion of lovers, not bound psychologically as merely mandatory marriage partners. Only then will our marriages and families experience the true ecstasy and joy intended for our functional daily lives. In living moment by moment, just as when lovers first met, dated, touched, kissed, and made love, can we continue to experience spontaneity and help free each other from the burden of any unhealthy dependency or insecure attachment of any kind. This requires that we first come to love and accept ourselves as we are, a theme that is repeatedly integrated in the preceding chapters. Healing ourselves first is ever the key before we can fully connect to our fellow beings.

With this brief example, I conclude with some final thoughts.

Know that there is no need for attaching any blame, remorse, or guilt in relation to our sexual nature and our relationships as they are today. I do offer a suggestion that men and women consider taking a positive lead role by emitting renewed loving signals, where the human heart can freshly respond to a loving resuscitation of a relationship that liberates each other more and possesses each other less each day. The path of deeper love will thus continue on for you as the role of giver and receiver become increasingly blurred, merging into one. In mutual love, we can at last leave old agendas and ledger sheets to dissolve into our holy oneness that paradoxically frees our individuality to shine. In this way, you will light up the world.

By being together, we can freely choose support each other's growth and release one another to fly daily before returning to our nests. If there is any competition, let it be that we compete to outlove each other, with daily expressions of how we value our partners. In simply loving one another first without expectation, all other blessings will follow.

The chapter concludes with this marital poem.

As my three daughters began to wed, I felt compelled to write about how love's earnest intentions might best be expressed in serving as a blessing to any lovers desiring to share their lives together as beloved partners. This poem intentionally points in a direction to rise above the often limiting paradigms regarding love as framed by both church, state, and cultural institutions. Simply put, these frameworks often promote illusory romantic notions of love to legalistic and fearful religious precepts that detract from free will and discolor the beautiful love that is everyone's birthright.

Love Is Perfect

So perfectly simple,
Transparently divine,
Transforming one's temple,
Passionately sublime.
So sacred is the feminine, blessed be a woman,
In balance with her masculine, forged a perfect union.
Equally holy is this masculine, blessed is a man,
Born from mother earth, she welcomes his reunion.

Penetrated hearts will free both spirit and souls,
Rebirthed by the womb, transformative love flows.
A pure reflection from the moon, her cycle all aglow,
The sun of God shines upon her, for his love to know.

Absorbed in God's lush garden, as sung by Solomon,
A goddess gives life, a breath of creative wisdom.
In this natural essence, heavens gifts did bestow,
Dive deep in loves oasis, rejoicing in the afterglow.

So simple is this sweetness, in sowing heaven's seed,
No need for detailed dogma, or complicated creed.
In love we were created, our natural state of being,
Beyond our world's illusions, love delivers our releasing.

So look beyond the veil, it is there for all to see,
By balancing our genders, engenders love to be.
Being in blessed union, delivers a birthright of liberty,
In the giving of oneself, one receives their divinity!

As we join in celebration, of our creator's loving gift,
Symbolizing our reunion, for all human hearts to uplift.
We all bless this one example of their mutual unity,
Reflecting loves healing potential, for all humanity.
With this single act, we witness one within two,
Loving energy attracts, our own lives to renew.
So bless you both, for a love that lights the way,
In this sacred moment when you say "I do" today.

Richard Francis Moore

Love is all perfecting,
Transparently divine,
Personally transcending,
Our saving grace for all time.

"*The first duty of love is to listen*" (Paul Tillich).

Reflections for Healing
(Your Optional Journal)

Chapter 9
Rhythms of Rumi and Songs of Solomon for the New Millennium
Understanding Sexuality and Healing

What observations caught your attention in this chapter?

Did you gain any new information or perspective on sexuality that you might further explore?

In regard to love, sexuality, and relationships, did this chapter offer new insights?

Did any poetic mediation prove helpful in any way?

Your Other Notes:

ACT III: THE FUTURE

A Declaration of Divinity

As each passing moment moves us into our future, it is no longer perceived as a place to fear but as a never-ending destination secured with a certainty grounded in love—a destiny reserved for us, created for us to be from the beginning of time and for all eternity. It is a place beyond the concept of time itself, a place where even our own understandings of physics short-circuits as time becomes immeasurable. This expansive eternity was born out of oneness, and our communion together remains our destiny. Here our human experience of incomprehensible individual diversity grows into our conscious choice to celebrate being together again!

All that remains is for us to exercise our free will as prayerful meditation triggers within a remembrance of who we were originally created to be. At that moment we can choose to reclaim our inheritance that awaits us as "we the people" choose to fulfill our promise of liberty and freedom for all, aka our promised land. We cannot return alone however, for a critical mass of individuals must first act to invite one and all for humanity to truly return as one people, "under God, indivisible, with liberty and justice for all." So it is that when all peoples have been made aware of this opportunity to freely choose to return home, we the people (all of us as a "chosen people") may proceed in unity. For this reason (and this again is from the highest authority), as we awaken, we are ever free to create the future. At such time, we will ultimately endorse *a declaration of divinity,* which has been born out of a common union with all creation, and we now choose to return to our original state of love! It is true that once upon a time, we had freely chosen to become independent of Eden. In our dreamlike fantasy, this is the fallen state that has been referred to in virtually every spiritual tradition; and those inspired scribes were not wrong in referring to our leaving paradise as entering our fallen state.

A fall from grace, yes, but neither a banishment nor punishment, but merely a free will choice to be . . . . well, independent of all things. A grand illusion it is, and it is really quite funny if you look back at it from this perspective, being that we have imagined we are separated from an omnipotent creator. This is an absolute impossibility as the created could not possibly separate themselves from their source of creation, and furthermore that our divine source/creator would ever abandon what was divinely created

194

in perfection. Thus it is that we have all participated in the grandest of Shakespearian-style stage plays. With great imagination, we have all acted out our roles quite convincingly in our dramatic tragic comedy of separation from God and from each other. Our constant reality is that we are all from one family, whether we believe it or not, embrace each other or not.

If one begins to trace back our family tree, you can see the various roles and stages of our shared journey. When reviewing, it becomes more apparent that our historical dependencies eventually led to declaring our natural independence, which lead us on a path of discovering our inevitable interdependence upon each other once more. Then lo and behold, the divine plan comes into view on a future sunrise. In the light of a new day, we begin to see our way forward to make our prodigal return home with the realization of our oneness, and in heightened awareness, we are invited to create new paradigms of understanding to *declare our divinity!*

While we are indeed in a fallen state, this remains only our momentary reality and does so only in the sense of our imagined separation from God, our superficial state of an experimental independent existence. Yes, the experience is most real, but more in the context of that theatrical stage on which we act out our lives. Even our perceived mortal enemies are only real because so many agree to act out our lives in this way. The obvious fact is that the entire human family cannot be enemies any more than god/goddess can deny us as his/her children. Nevertheless, the show must go on, so let us proceed to see how our actions unfold to their inevitable conclusion. Like a good movie, we may sense the impending finish, but we must all follow through by staying to view the ending and finish living out the experience that we ourselves chose to start. One cannot find peace until they first see that it has been one hell of a delusion we have created, and one that we have all willingly participated in!

Entering our future we must now remember in times of fear and uncertainty that our ultimate and inevitable destiny is to recall and reenter our original community of oneness. Our current state of cyclical conflict remains only as a fleeting creation behind the theater curtains of our own illusory reality. Here we project a temporary state of our imagination as the movie flickers those false images on fragmented beams of light. Even as a film can make us cry or laugh, our self-inflicted and chosen physical reality intensely hurts us all in real time! No our chosen sufferings do not seem like any imaginary illusion, but our joyous future will ultimately unveil itself to each of us as we consciously choose our paradigms of tomorrow. In a most real sense, it is just a kiss away!

Too simplistic or farfetched you say?

Let's try one more short explanation. Recall how in one brief historical moment the world was no longer imagined to be flat. At this moment in time mankind similarly remains in a spell of self-fulfilling apocalyptic paradigms. By our failing to understand the illusory nature of this physical life as only relatively true, we have clouded creations clear vision for humanity by merely blocking our eyes with our own hands. It is as if we are all children playing pretend roles (temporarily tragic though they may be) in the backyard just outside our parents' view. Similarly, creation/creator patiently and lovingly awaits our return home with open arms, and like the infamous prodigal son, he/she has their arms wide open for all sons and daughters to return to the safety and bliss of eternal, inexhaustible, and unconditional love! It is akin to the entertaining and beloved *Wizard of Oz* which gifted us with a prophetic message that we have always had the power to return home. If you need more serious affirmations, you can read how both science and spirituality support this in the semantics of their own language.

Thus we move into the book's final chapter with a truly *divine declaration* that all of creation is free to reunite, consciously choosing to reconnect our individual diversity with our incomprehensible original oneness as humankind!

We hold these truths to be self-evident—that all creation was created by one divine source; thus, we are all endowed by the Creator as divine loving beings. By our very nature, we are born to be free and fearless, happy in our liberation we remain holy and healthy, understanding that we are all interconnected eternally! We now reclaim this joy as our birthright and inheritance!

Seeing the Synchronicity

In communion,
An inevitable reunion,
In communication,
Our reunion sets us free.

Perpetual motion at a dizzying pace,
Produces gravity in a balanced place,
Providing cyclical positions in seasonal space,
With the speed of light, we can now retrace,
Witnessing creations original face,
The eternal moment of the human race.

Enlightenment shines from the cosmic glow,
Destined as one, in both body and soul.
True liberty invites us to rejoin the wise,
As *in the beginning* we were all synchronized.

With billions of people on the planet, and each one holding different beliefs on innumerable subjects, it appears futile to continue playing the ancient game of identifying who our immediate enemies are. It seems insane to be insecure about others who see life differently than we do since no two individuals will ever agree on everything!

The following poem was a playful attempt to either identify enemies or at least resign ourselves to a new understanding that our differences can serve a positive purpose in balancing our world of apparent opposites. In this place of opposite viewpoints, it is no longer in anyone's best interest in continuing with a paradigm that equates differences as reasons for conflict and war.

For example, I have no quarrel with the instructions of Jesus for us to "love thy enemies as thyself." I also think that Francis of Assisi expressed this same wisdom by simply encouraging us to begin our divine renewal by merely making an effort to genuinely "understand others before seeking to be understood." This is where our perceived enemies may at last perish before us once and for all, not by violence, but with understanding.

Artwork by Jimi Tutko

The Enemy

Know thy enemy!
This is critically important were told!
Preachers quote prophets,
Profiting from an apocalypse foretold.

Who is the enemy?
Is it the Mid-East, Palestine, Israel, Iran, Pakistan, Afghanistan, Syria, or Iraq?
Is it communist China, or North Korea, or Vietnam?
Perhaps it is it Russia, or Bosnia, Croatia, or Turkey?
Maybe the European Union for their economic threat and their past World War histories?
Lest we forget, it could be Cuba, Grenada, or Venezuela, or Mexicans to the south, or even those contrarian Canadians to the north?

Are they kings, czars, despots, dictators, sultans, sheiks, chiefs, premiers, prime ministers, or presidents?
Certainly socialists, Marxist, communists, royalists, or tyrants, and terrorists?
Are they Hindus, Muslims (Sunni or Shiite), Bhuddists, Christians (Catholic, Protestant, Evangelical, Mormon, AME, or . . .)?
Or is it the humanists, secularist, scientists, atheists, or agnostics?

Are they residing in our own country?
Could the enemy be social liberals or hateful Nazis types concealed in Conservative clothing?
Are corporate CEOs in control of Congress, justices, the White House, and other nations?
Is it the illegal immigrants, Hispanics, blacks, or the independent nations of our native tribes?
Or is it the old powers, Free Masons, Illuminati, Opus Dei, or Rothschild banks calling the shots?
Do capitalist barons, multinational corporations, and colonial Caucasians still control power?
Or is it the military industrial complex we were forewarned about, or arms dealers fostering ever new worldwide conflicts?
Is it individual nations or the United Nations?
Are our enemies aliens and UFOs in the end, manipulating our worlds chaos?

Who is the enemy I ask you! Is it
A) One of the above (if so, which one(s) please specify _____)?
B) Some of the above?
C) None of the above, or all of the above?
D) Is it all of us?

Or is the enemy mythical, or perhaps the one reflecting in our mirrors
harboring hatred each morning?

History cautions us to know thy enemy,
This repetitive reasoning can help us to see,
That by translating your fears into hate and hostility,
You will never defeat them, preventing oneself from being set free,
For in simple awareness of each other, there lies our future liberty!
Putting the Brakes upon destruction, we break the cycle.

A Day in the Eternal Moment

In the depths of a winter's day,
I drifted with the winds,
I heard your voice, I smiled,
I saw you face, I grinned,
I heard your laugh, I laughed,
Absorbing your humor, I became happier,
Feeling your spirit, I was energized,
Sensing our kinship, I was warmed.

Spring breezes are warmly welcomed,
With growth and enlightenment each day,
Like a lifelong friend returning,
The nature of friendship is reassuring,
Divine yet devilishly delightful,
Humorously human, mystically marvelous.
An imperfect perfection,

So abundant and plentiful.
Expressing human nature to one and all,
Spring's equinox also proves paradoxical,
Just the opposite of our images of our fall.

Playing amid summer's long light,
Interdependence freely flows,
Internally and externally,
In this cycle where everything grows.

Our Independence flowers for loving reasons,
Guiding our destiny in ever changing seasons.
Interdependence is an eternal blessing for all,
Producing a harvest that sustains us when we fall.

Artwork by Jimi Tutko

Fabric of Friendship

In the ever unfolding gift of friendship,
I send out intentions with no strings to attach,
Desiring only to share freely with you that fabric,
With which my essential nature has been strung,
Reconnecting in ways, of which other's have sung.

By sharing these threads of my friendship,
You may appreciate the various ways I have been woven.
Hopefully understanding the exposure of my soul,
Beyond the appearances of my torn and frayed portions,
My threadbare imperfections, are merely mortal distortions.

May the hand of friendship mend so many loose ends,
Bonds strengthen, as hands touch with heartfelt amends.
Through such bonds, we are restored and made whole,
So our fragile friendships, may hearten body and soul.

Reaching out to others, reconnects our friendly reunion,
Interweaving and intertwining, in uncommon communion.
Giving and receiving, extended hands for further mending,
As all of our friendships, are truly never ending.

"I feel within me a peace above all earthly dignities, a still and quiet conscience" **(William Shakespeare).**

Chapter 10

Perspectives and Paradigms

Understanding Paradise Found

In each moment, we all have stories to share and write,
Healing each other, without judging wrong or right,
Beyond gender, God-Goddess bless us with insight,
In balance we create in divine love and light.

This book began by acknowledging that the personal circumstances of everyone's journey through life are uniquely different. From the moment of birth, our chronological age adds to the many contrasts of residing in different climates and countries, each with their own religious and cultural influences. It is inevitable that we all naturally view life from our own distinctive perspectives. How could it be any other way? Given our diverse circumstances, let me briefly address how a process of personal healing contains the potential for claiming your inner peace. If you decide to pursue it, you stand to discover a formerly lost paradise once again found.

The title *The Paradigm Prophecies: Reflections for Healing* is both an affirmation and an invitation to proclaim power over your own life, an ultimate reality that remains ever available to all. Your true nature is innately powerful, and appearances to the contrary are some of the darkest illusions we can live with. Our world's illusions have until now conspired to construct the prevailing paradigms that maintain the status quo of our cultural, religious, and social institutions around our world. Such powerful foundational paradigms often lock us into repetitious patterns that rather than free us, they can entrap both body and soul. When we willingly step back and unemotionally observe this dynamic, we can begin to better understand everyone's legitimate values and perspectives.

In the simple act of genuinely understanding others (no need to agree or capitulate), we present ourselves with a gift. It is the gift of "getting others," and with genuine understanding, we free ourselves to be capable of reevaluating the relevancy of our governing paradigms. From this perch one can begin better comprehending the rapid changes now unfolding before us, and learn from each other. As previously mentioned, recall how humanity once insisted that we lived upon a flat world with a sun revolving around us as the center of the universe. Again, as our world changes daily, an ancient question also beckons us to consider, what long-held belief is about to change next? With conscious understanding, we can all create new paradigms to guide us back to our paradise found.

In order for any single individual to rise above conforming to the powerful pressure of public paradigms (the granddaddy of all peer pressures), they must first become aware of perspectives outside of what they have been taught and exposed to. This is where the personal power within can help us, and with courage can help free humanity from their own trappings to pursue liberty and freedom for all.

Each new understanding equips a person with new insights. These rays of light can empower any individual to awaken from their wilderness experience of a perceived separation from their divinity. The individual rays of light will similarly help guide humanity to their growth and reawakening. As one individual at a time awakens to the original power implanted within them, it will collectively build and contribute to a synergy that will help heal the greater human family and our world. As we continue to gain a more universal understanding of each other, we all become informal healers in very natural ways. At some point, human awareness and understanding will reach a certain threshold (aka a tipping point), when healing will correspondingly accelerate in a manner similar to how fast history witnessed the American Revolution unfold or, more recently, how our technological capacities have unimaginably sped up our global connectivity. Such speedy paradigm shifts will soon be unveiled as humanity exponentially grows socially, emotionally, spiritually, and beyond.

As each individual takes time to reach out and understand the viewpoints of others, a healthy energy is released. This energy helps fuel our personal rediscovering of our divinity, and as we remember our origins, paradise will be found. The books affirmation of awakening oneself to the personal power within, necessarily suggests that you will first find your paradise individually and slowly be rejoined with all of creation in declaring our shared divinity! This can only begin within oneself, all else and all others will follow. An important distinction however is realize that while individual consciousness needs to come first, faith that any individual leader can deliver us and save the world singlehandedly is misplaced. Any leaders' efforts to change the world (by subliminally relieving us of our responsibility to think and act for ourselves) will ultimately prove to be a futile and fruitless expenditure of energy. Our world however can indeed be saved, but only when a critical mass of individuals become aware that they have the power to collectively change the future, *together*! Yes, leaders have a role to play, but in the final analysis they are always a mirror of the populace at each moment in time.

To be clear, I am not propagating some new age cliché idealism, nor am I looking through rose-colored glasses to view our world with a Pollyanna-like fantasy. This is not about any naive pacifism that asks, "Can't we all just get along with each other?" On the contrary, I am realistically conceding and confirming that conflicts and ailments will continue to remain a harsh reality in our current world. Our pain is all too real and hurts deeply at every level of our senses. The fact is change come grudgingly as the forces of the status quo will resist any change that threatens their controlling power. Change is often not pretty! What I am saying, however, is that we each possess a healing power within that can profoundly change our understandings, and only then will our future global circumstances positively follow.

While we all need others to occasionally aid us in our healing (ranging from highly trained specialists at one end of the spectrum to more mystical practitioners at the other) we will always remain our best advocates for our own healing. Our positive intentions will attune us to our internal GPS for healing, with which we were born. The words of Jesus, Buddha, and Mohammed all affirmed that one needs to look within to find enlightenment, not outward to others. Jesus added that if we only had faith the size of a mustard seed, then we ourselves could move mountains. A key point in many religious texts and traditions around the world has consistently been that we were miraculously created in the image and likeness of the Creator, and we need not seek out a leader or intermediary for solutions to our salvation. Since we can all directly access the divine within us, we are in fact, all responsible not only for our own actions but also the outcomes born out of our religions, cultures, nations, and any groups to which we may personally belong.

This, of course, has never gone over well with the guardians of institutional dogma. The truth of this irony does not need to devalue religion, for it can also be positive and helpful, but it is an equally sobering reminder that we should never forfeit our own responsibility or relinquish moral leadership to others. We cannot excuse ourselves for giving blind allegiance to any authority as this complicit arrangement has historically lead to much tragedy, hurt, and heartache for humanity.

The truth is that our institutions and all their paradigms can only change when each of us takes responsibility for the groups we claim membership to. Whatever the belief system, if we belong to it, we share some responsibility for the outcomes. When we forfeit our influence by passively accepting the dictates or absolutes of others, we can fully expect our world to continue on with the same destructive conflicts. Our world needs a new declaration of our shared divinity, for this is where true freedom and liberty reside. In the end, our world needs everyone to declare and speak their truth while authentically respecting divergent and even opposite outlooks. As Francis of Assisi (himself a veteran of the Crusades) advised us long ago, the healing process requires we must first reach out to understand other's way of life.

Without genuine understanding, we only create new dogmas, new righteous dictates, and new ideologies, all of which only recreate the same old conflicts via new wars. Healing can never emerge from such a righteous and authoritarian approach, be it religious or political. Even as I earnestly share my experiences, I am not advocating my thoughts to represent some new doctrine. I am not a preacher or politician, but I am simply giving you observations as the keys to your vehicle along with some suggested routes you may drive upon during the journey mapped within your own heart. Here you can find your own peace and healing and come to experience the truth of your own destiny. The world needs everyone to find their own way, (not by other authorities), and in doing so, we will all fulfill our divinely human destiny together.

The progressions contained in these chapters provided an informal process that is simple yet comprehensive, practical and mystical for healing both the physical and metaphysical dimensions of our being. As we are all progressing along on our own journey, may the intentions of each reader be blessed as you observe and come to understand the eternal truth implanted within you. May it heal you and all those you touch in your life until we all return to that paradise found anew!

So in conclusion, let us consider this aspect of our duality (or paradoxical nature) of our human-divine essence as has been previously cited. What better way to illustrate this dichotomy than to summarize with both serious themes and intentionally silly examples? Amazing healing can occur when a smile is seen or laughter is heard in the midst of the serious circumstances that surround the conflicts of life. The intent here is for us to resist ever taking any aspect of life so seriously (including ourselves) as to risk forfeiting the balance of our laughter and good humor.

Our humanity can be very funny and healing if we but notice it! If there were a Paradox Hall of Fame, slapstick humor would have a prominent place in it as we observe how comedy is often found in the most common occurrences of our daily life. Some examples date back a century to the *Three Stooges* to the more recent television sitcom *Seinfeld* in a show purportedly about nothing. Each presented us with situations typical in our daily circumstances that helped us laugh at ourselves.

In many ways the popularity of these comics succeeded because so many of us related to the absurdity of the petty problems we all deal with and share in. Interestingly, we usually laugh louder when observing our friends slipping on that banana peel or even when we happen to be the victims of a fall we can often laugh at ourselves (after recovering our composure and swallowing our pride, of course). If we are able to drop the ego-centered reasons for any embarrassment, we free ourselves to step back and see that our clumsy moments pretty much resemble the lives of others. These comical moments are reminders of accepting our common human bonds, and they could help us have more empathy for one another by also demonstrating and reassuring us of our common divinity. If it is true that "fact is often stranger than fiction," it may be similarly true that comedy contains a more accurate portrayal of humankind than our tragically serious historical chronicles.

"Humor is the great thing, the saving thing. The minute it crops up, all our irritations and resentments slip away and a sunny spirit takes their place." (Mark Twain)

From this perspective, we should laugh heartily at the illusion of our purported separation from an eternal creation/creator. This assertion is the mother of all oxymoron's as separation from our source of creation is simply impossible! From the mouth of babes we are all in this together—forever.

"God said he loves everyone, but   *"God asked me to tell you she is not angry."*
I can't count that high."

Photos by Richard F. Moore

Comic Relief

I have good news and bad, the comic will say,
Eternal love is ours; we have no hell to pay.
Not just good news, God's good humor is great,
Unless your own judgment, imagines a hellish fate.

Only bad news is doomed to die, so you just let it be,
As divine creations we will always be loved eternally.
Created in God's image, our true reality show,
Brothers and sisters in our human family to know.

Forgiveness will freeze fires, while cold blood finally thaws,
What is freely forgiven inspires, overcoming theological flaws.

Observing Shakespeare's tragedies in our daily scenes,
Stand-up human dramas produce sit-comical schemes.
For we are already forgiven, for each act we install,
For the dye it is cast, love's last chapter includes all.

Thus Good News for one, and good news for all,
We were just kidding ourselves, in big ways and small.
Since the joke was on us all, no more need to save face,
beloved in each moment, in our ever saving grace

"Gratitude"

Happiness is already here,
Emitting outward from your sphere.
You release it daily with each beatitude,
An unleashing of joy, births a new attitude,
Renewing a lease on life, with love and gratitude,

Revealing happiness and humor are in your sight,
Belong to you as your holy birthright,
For you are already a divine heir
Manifesting health, is a gift we share.

"Ever In The Ether"

Ever loving, ever present,
Everlasting, evermore.
Everyone, every instance,
Every instant, every moment.

Every grain of sand, every blade of grass,
Every strand hair counted, every being ever loved.

Every trouble surmounted,
Every solution pending,
Ever receiving, ever sending,
Ever more loving, never ending.
Every corner of the universe exists as one,
For one, for all...........healing everyone, forever in the ether!

"Oneness"
One expanding universe, One creation,
One synchronization, One explanation,
One divine intelligence,
One spiritual and scientific convergence,
One remembrance, one loving redundance.

Artwork by Jimi Tutko

One communion, One single source,
One eternal moment, One healing,
Only forgiveness,
Only Oneness.
Only Love.
One universal truth,
One universe, One love, One verse,
Oneness!

Parental Paradise Found
With the sun now setting,
Upon our parenting role.
No thought of regretting,
No lamenting of the soul.

Always in relationship,
In a revolutionary new form.
In recreated friendship,
A recreation thus born.

Recreation as in being playful,
Released from a life so full,
Dipping into a sea of tranquility.
No womb to bear more responsibility.

Free to see, to hear, and to fully feel,
Renewing old, and new friendships with zeal,
Tasting goodness, inhaling all of life's scents,
Savoring all blessings and spontaneous moments

A Bridge to Eden

Consider crossing over that proverbial bridge,
That space which once appeared as an impassable chasm.
Peering down into those still waters below,
Reflect upon those mirrored images of our unity.
Seeing with calm, the clarity of our pooled existence,
Observing all that we share in common together.

So courageously cross over,
Joining with others from another side of life,
To share the treasures you have to give them,
And discover the gifts they wait for you to receive!

Observing so much water passing under the bridge,
Each drop flowing in unison into the stream of life,
Similarly discovering we share one human family,
Sharing one planet, one solar system,
Sharing one universe, one cosmos,
One inseparable, infinite, and incomprehensible joy!

Worth Repeating

You do not need to relive the past,
We do not need to repeat the past!

As our problems are often of our own making,
We can resolve them, and release our forsaking.

Disease, starvation, scarcity and war,
Need not continue, as we explore,
New ways to renew, a way to restore,
A healthy future, as it was long before.

With a conscious commitment we can be bound,
On our journey in progress, to paradise found!
So repeat to yourself, let your voice resound,
It is worth repeating, a road to paradise is found.
You can free yourself, be free at last,
Thank God almighty, you're freed from the past.

Three voices,

. . . from three traditions,

. . . from one divine source.

"And mankind is naught but a single nation" (Quran 2:213).

"We must become the change we want to see in the world" (Mohandas Gandhi).

"Truly, I say to you, unless you turn and become like children, you will never enter the kingdom of heaven" (Matthew 18:1–3).

We must again become like children . . . God's children, remembering we have always been one human family, and ever it shall be!

A man, a woman, a balance . . . *Amen*!

Photo by Richard F. Moore & Mary Hazel

Reflections for Healing
(Your Optional Journal)

Chapter 10

Perspectives and Paradigms
Understanding Paradise Found

What observations caught your attention in this chapter?

Have you noted any new perspectives that you wish to explore further?

Have you gained any helpful insights or understanding(s) in regard to this chapters topics?

Did any poetic mediation prove beneficial to seeing potentially new paradigms for helping humanity?

Your Other Notes:

Epilogue

Understanding Unity & Liberty

"If you want others to be happy, practice compassion.
If you want to be happy, practice compassion."
—The Dalai Lama

As our final act is yet to be written, we will continue to be shaped by the collective energy of our individual conscious decisions. What will each of us discover and declare as newly revealed truths in this century, this new millennium? What new paradigm(s) will we choose to build our future foundations upon in order to fulfill the infinite destiny for which we were created?

Recognizing that every one of us is at a different place in their life journey, this book offers a person a safe, private and informal process for self-guided healing. Freed from the internal and external pressures of differing belief systems it is presented as but one tool, one approach to help assist anyone seeking clarity upon their path of personal destiny. In order to support anyone interested in further using this as a working tool, I have provided a summary worksheet that includes a checklist of the major themes at the end of the book. Listen and let your inner voice be your guide as you quietly permit your answers to come from within. As you do this, enjoy the miracle of the creative process and everlasting journey we are all sharing in together!

Healing Recap: Some Closing Perspectives Are Worth Rephrasing

A key suggestion of these healing reflections encourages one to identify certain aspects of life that you passionately disagree with, or issues you simply do not understand. For instance, you may be perplexed how another individual or institution could ever embrace a particular belief. These points of contention can often threaten our beliefs and leave us feeling insecure if we permit them to foster fear and suspicion. Unchecked in the extreme, these feelings can produce anger with the potential to escalate into hatred and violence.

214

Like every aspect of life, fear, suspicion, and anger can actually serve a momentary positive purpose, but in excess, these reflex reactions can grow like cancer cells and overtake our healthy functioning. Arguably, one could make a case that we need to identify and be aware of these triggers in advance before they lead us into negative extremes that can become root causes for many human illnesses. For these reasons, the book stresses the importance of making your most earnest efforts to identify and understand viewpoints that, for whatever reasons, befuddle you or you are vehemently opposed to.

The purpose of this effort again is not to try and change your beliefs or values but to empower yourself by genuinely grasping how, what, and why others believe and act the way they do. While this process begins as a mental construct, it simultaneously requires our heart's earnest commitment to emotionally understand that which is contrary to our own belief systems. There is no debate to be won here, but personal freedom, liberty, and healing are born out of true 'understanding'.

"Imagination is more important than knowledge."
—Albert Einstein

Here is where you can experience how new perspectives can lead us to imagine potential new paradigms for healing ourselves, our world, and the physical planet itself. As suggested in chapter 10, picture for a moment that Mother Earth was once paradise. Now begin to envision and comprehend how our own healing actions will lead us to rediscover this paradise as newly found. Like a newborn baby slowly lifting their eyelids, any blurred vision will clear to see this truth as if it were hidden in plain sight all along.

As an author, I do express the truth of my own life experience, yet I have no desire to sell any new doctrine, dogma, or righteous creed as billions of individuals all have their unique path, viewpoints, and special gifts to contribute to humankind. An important assertion I do intend is that it behooves everyone to make a positive contribution to our own healing. In the prologue of this book, I essentially extended an invitation for the reader to take a personal mental journey through the course of their own life from many different vantage points. I encourage every reader to imagine looking down upon your life from outer space, through the clouds, or from a perch on a high mountain peak. Now invert this image by going underground to peer up through a glass floor as if you were viewing some aquarium exhibit. Such an approach affords one an opportunity to safely explore opposite sides of any issue, and pursue new thoughts and insights on healing. By privately reflecting upon your life and others', you might discover many aspects of life that we do share in common. Since our personal paths can often appear as conflicting, paradoxical, and irreconcilably different, we need to carefully examine how we are also interconnected with common desires, goals, needs, and hopes that we share as a human race.

Speaking of the human race, one of the book's secondary intentions is encouragement to stop our "human racing," if you will, by slowing down and quieting ourselves. Our driving chronically fast can cause us to accidentally miss important signs and meaningful scenery while silencing many sweet sounds to closed windows as we race down life's path. With extreme speed, we can become blind, deaf, and dumb and needlessly risk crashing the very cultures, countries, economies, and continents we profess to love. Individual recklessness ultimately threatens the health of our entire world. We all are well advised to consider tapping on our brakes and slow things down to check where we are going in such a hurry, and why? By learning to pause in silence, we open ourselves to the gift of differing perspectives on just where our individual journeys began and where they intersect for the whole of humanity.

In this spirit, the book offers road maps and poses fundamental questions for each individual reader to answer in private.

- Going forward, are there any facets of life you might choose to consider changing to better serve your personal health and well-being?
- Can you identify specific aspects of this world that you feel could be improved upon to benefit all of humankind?
- Are there teachings you were raised with from your culture, religion, or country that you have come to question the validity of over time?

These are but a few summary questions designed to help us see for ourselves that there is no one among us who has not made course corrections during any serious journey in their life. As we mature over the decades, we are given defining moments for us to freely decide upon the desired destination of our own journey. Such opportunities are missed when we blindly replicate someone else's idea of who and what they think we should be. When we thoughtlessly repeat our traditional behaviors we are expected to live up to, one can run the risk of missing many joys in their life experience. These competing tensions of making course corrections versus maintaining the social status quo help explain our human inclinations to

- look for leaders to follow;
- form governments to fight for; and

○ organize religions to provide us an easy set of "absolute" and uniform answers for our existence and agreed upon terms of salvation.

These often well-intentioned designs to provide some stability can be tempting, as creating some human uniformity certainly holds a welcome attraction in a confusing and chaotic world. Ultimately, many of these simplistic pretenses are exposed as complicit constructs that prove superficial and, in the end, fail to satisfy the depths of our heart and soul. One such example is the classic creed of presenting only one religion as true while rendering all others as false. The irony in this is that this proclamation is what most religions actually have in common.

Interestingly, even when specific groups or populations give the appearance of conformity, it usually only represents a homogenous facade. In reality, mass conformity is like an adult version of teen peer pressure that can appeal to the insecurity of our own egos. This tactic is socially powerful, but in the end, it remains a futile social coercion that fails to satisfy our intuitive truth, just as our adolescent experiences once did. Invariably these sometimes well intended efforts for controlling the masses are merely shortcuts we have all participated in at some level. The problem is they come fraught with elements of those complicit compromises that limit our thinking and our healthy fulfillment as individuals. This is why we all share some responsibility for the faulty foundations upon which we have built our churches, institutions, nations, and social groups. Organizing ourselves can be an extremely positive initiative if we choose to build upon a truthful paradigm. Since we are each responsible for the actions of our groups, our considerations of many perspectives are critical for the healthy functioning of all.

Unfortunately, the historical fruits of these labors to organize ourselves in groups have more often created increased separation and conflict rather than inclusive resolution, divisiveness more than unity, hatred over love, and death over life! For this reason, I have repeatedly stated that my written observations do not represent yet another new creed or righteous belief system. Knowing this, the reader of this book and the world can be relieved that I am *not* presenting myself as some new guru, prophet, or leader in any way. I am, however, the proud author of these inspired messages I have been given to assist in human healing!

The true value of this book is to help empower yourself and foster greater understanding of how your individuality is a divine gift that can also unify and heal one another. Only you can choose to explore and discover your unique contribution to benefit yourself and, in so doing, help humankind to experience both individual liberty and unity at the same time.

My consistent emphasis is that you possess the keys for your own journey, not me, nor any earthly authority. This is a divine gift to one and all, and I am merely another messenger (as are each of us in our own way). If you have gleaned any beneficial lessons from my writing, remember that they are, in truth, a collective mirror image garnered from thousands of conversations I have been blessed to hear from hundreds of people I was privileged to have known. Yes, you too are a messenger, as none of us are of greater or less importance than another. Be wary of those who either elevate themselves or try to diminish another.

A closing reminder before leaving you to pursue your healing journey is to remember that not one of us is always correct or in error, never totally heroic or forever humbled. The truth is that we can all grow from each other's experiences when we make mistakes or succeed by making important contributions in our sphere of influence! Since we all get opportunities to play varying roles on the stage of life, the question is how will you freely choose to contribute and participate in our increasingly shared future together on a planet desperately in need of healing? It doesn't take a prophet to predict change is coming, but it does take visionaries to help create paradigms for a healthier future.

In the final analysis, unity is not beneficial if it is merely a byproduct of societal coercion and superficial conformity. True freedom and liberty for the human spirit must be born out of respect for individuals, who at the same time have awoken to understand what we all share in common together. So it is when as we become aware that our individual differences contribute to a healthy unity, the human family will cease to be at war with each other.

Paradigm Prophecies

Describing

Do you subscribe to the notion that God has spoken to us over time?
If so, do you think his or her *final messages* were *all* communicated to us millenniums ago?
Do you think the written word contained in scriptures, scrolls, alongside oral traditions of many faiths described *all* the insights we were ever meant to learn from?

Do we, after all, ever stop learning and growing in our education, or in our own daily lives?
Do you not think that other prophets and inspired writers continue to be among us to this day?

Do you not think an omnipotent all-loving creator, can communicate in innumerable methods beyond our limited thinking?

Is it not possible that the universal source of life can speak to us in indescribable ways?
Is it so difficult to believe the divine still speaks to us in any number of ways this very day?
Describe your own answers . . . Privately for yourself!

Scribing

Be assured you already possess this ancient knowledge,
It is already inscribed within each of us.
Encrypted in our intuitive wisdom,
A prescription for a healthy humanity.

Freshly inspired I have scribed a rephrasing of old words,
Fulfilling the language of many previous tongues,
Ancient voices spoke loudly to awaken my sight,
Calling upon me to write both by day and night.

For nearly two decades I wrote without ceasing,
Accumulating poems with prose increasing.
These collective words have grown in volume and inspiration,
With a *breath of fresh air*, they provide resuscitation.

I am revived, a renewed re-creation,
Remembering we are all divine creations,
With no desire for elevation, nor saintly separation,
I offer no egotistical assertions, or rationalizations.
We need only listen to *our truth* in heart and mind,
Assured that everyone is invited to participate in kind.

Prescribing

As the creator and universal intelligence continues communicating with us,
It seems quite natural that this is also accomplished through each other as fellow divine beings.
Just observe our modern world, sense the angels, as enlightened beings increasingly abound.

Observe the wealth of inspired new spiritual writings being published around the globe,
All prescribing our healthy future path in fulfilling our destiny together.

Whether it is the discovery of more ancient scrolls, providing new insights,
Or the end of a Mayan calendar, marking time for the dawning of a new light,
Be it the realization of our old apocalyptic patterns,
Or in contrast to our increasing awareness of each other,
We are increasingly embraced and encircled in an emerging global consciousness.

Listen and you can hear a new chapter unfolding for humanity in our present times.
Of course, free will is always the rule, as we freely use both our reason and rhyme.
The choice is always yours, when it comes to changing any historical pattern,
As you may take a new road home, returning by the light of your inner lantern.

Faulty foundations invariably crumble, while new paradigms of understanding will necessarily be constructed. May we choose to build them upon a solid foundation of respect and love of liberty for all.

In closure I offer a rephrasing of the texts most repeated and powerful keyword to healing, which is: ***understanding***!

Another way of grasping the simple but elusive significance of your healing power, try viewing it in this way. To truly understand emotionally, intellectually, pragmatically, and spiritually, one must step back with a mindset of detached observation. Here you can simply notice what is, and why it is. No need to judge, argue, agree or disagree. Such observing can produce a deep understanding, and help anyone to awaken to insights long hidden to us by our own indoctrinations. Again one need not abandon their own path or opinions, but with such understandings one will live a more informed and conscious existence. From an enlightened awareness of life as it was and is, you will find a new healing power within, a force to help you, your immediate family and indirectly the world in which you live. Herein lies our true liberty.

Thus it is, that in our ever changing physical world, old paradigms will fade as we better observe and understand our true nature within. As paradigms end, (one must not look back with "rose colored glasses", as our history has in reality been far from ideal) remember that it is always presenting an opportunity for a new beginning. The question is always, what shall we co-create together consciously, no longer by default?

The End..., as we begin anew......

The Paradigm Prophecies
Optional Summary Worksheet
(For possible use on your own ongoing healing journey)

After contemplating so many cross-sections of human life, you still may feel overwhelmed and asking a basic question: "How do I proceed to access my healing power within?" Not surprisingly, it will be different for every individual since we all decide to seek and discover our internal power and true freedom in our own time and our own way. To help, I have left below a list of topics from the book that might help guide you upon your own journey of rebirth, renewal, and flourishing. For some, it is a slow unfolding while others report an enlightenment experience.

Only you can choose to discover answers for healing. May this book serve as a helpful guide.

1) First remember the value in choosing to have an open mind by *observing* other *perspectives* with a goal of *understanding*. (No need to agree, just truly understand.)
2) As you seek new understanding on life, reflect on the context of *past, present, and future* in both beneficial and detrimental contexts.
3) Revisit the natural progressions maturing in life including *dependency, independence*, and *interdependence*, taking note on how these can help our health, or hurt us.
4) These initial steps help us face the *contradictions* of our being human as opposite truths simultaneously exist in our world. We need to positively manage these polarizing forces in balance, or risk being injured from their potentially conflicting outcomes.
5) Drawing upon your own experience, answer the following.
   a. List a totally unique personal experience of yours that no one else has had. _____?
   b. List an important personal moment that others have also likely experienced._____?
   c. List an event that was shared by a community, be it global, national, or local._____?

6) You may also find it useful to review any notes you made at the end of each chapter.
Chapter 1 - In the Darkness of Illusions: Understanding First Exposures
Chapter 2 - Early in the Journey: Understanding the Silence

"Health is worth more than learning." —Thomas Jefferson

Other Resources

In appreciation to the many special people who have influenced, inspired, and fostered my healthy growth, I have provided the following five appendices *(A-E)*. These resources offer helpful recommendations ranging from authors, books, related Web sites, inspiring musical selections, and alternative therapies that I have personally benefited from. You will find that some of these resources have been directly quoted or referenced within this book, yet all of them have positively contributed to my own healing path at one time or another. I share them for your bibliographical information as well as a potential source of encouragement, and blessing upon the path of your own life journey.

Blessings always!

Richard Francis Moore

APPENDIX A

(Authors and Books That Have Positively Influenced Healing in My Life)
****

Bach, Richard - *Illusions*
Barthlow, Jerry - *Peace Soup*
Beckwith, Michael Bernard - *The Life Visioning Process*
Buechner, Frederick - *The Sacred Journey*
Byrne, Rhonda - *The Secret*
Carey, Ken - *The Third Millennium and the Starseed Transmissions*
Chopra, Deepak - *Reinventing the Body, Resurrecting the Soul*
Deida, David - *Finding God Through Sex*
Emoto, Masaru - *The Hidden Messages in Water*
Fox, M. & Sheldrake, R - *The Physics of Angels*
Fromm, Erich - *The Art of Loving*
Gafni, Marc - *The Mystery of Love*
Gandhi, Mohandas K. - *The Story of My Experiments with Truth*
Hartong, Leo - *Awakening to the Dream*
Hawkins, David RMD, PhD - *Power vs. Force*
Hay, Louise - *You Can Heal Your Life*
Hicks, Esther and Jerry - *Ask and It Is Given: The Teachings of Abraham*
Hildegard of Bingen - *Secrets of God*
Hubbard, Barbara Marx - *Revelation: A Message of Hope for the New Millennium*
Katz, Jon - *Running to the Mountain: A Midlife Adventure*
Kendall, Elizabeth - *American Daughter: Discovering My Mother*
King, Martin Luther Jr. - *The Strength to Love*
Kingma, Daphne Rose - *The Future of Love*
Lamott, Anne - *All New People*
Leloup, Jean-Yves - *The Gospel of Mary Magdalene*
Linn, Denise - *Sacred Space*
MacKenzie, Gordon - *Orbiting the Giant Hairball*
McTaggart, Lynne-*The Intention Experiment*
Myss, Caroline, PhD- *Anatomy of the Spirit*
Null, Gary Ph.D. - *Natural Healing Encyclopedia*
Pagels, Elaine - *The Gnostic Gospels*
Prophet, Elizabeth Claire - *The Lost Teachings of Jesus*
Renard, Gary R. - *The Disappearance of the Universe*
Richardson, Diana -*The Heart of Tantric Sex*
Rumi - *Love Poems* (Edited by Deepak Chopra)

Schucman, Helen - *A Course in Miracles*
Schweitzer, Albert - *Reverence for Life*
Siegel, Bernie S. MD - *Peace, Love, & Healing*
Starbird, Margaret -*The Goddess in the Gospels*
Tolle, Eckhart - *A New Earth, Awakening to Your Life's Purpose*
Virtue, Doreen Ph.D. - *Archangels & Ascended Masters: A Guide to Healing*
Walsch, Neale Donald - *Conversations with God* (+ many others)
Williamson, Marianne - *Enchanted Love: The Mystical Power of Intimate Relationships*
Yonika, Maya - *No Mud, No Lotus*
Young, Wm. Paul - *The Shack*

The religious texts utilized in my writings included the following:

The Bhagavad Gita
The Bible
The Book of Mormon
The Quran
The Tao Te Ching (Lao Tzu)
The Torah

APPENDIX B

(Holistic and Alternative Therapies, and practices I Have Personally Utilized and Benefited From)
****

Acupuncture
Akashic reading
Aroma therapy
Astrology
Breath work
Chinese medicine
Chiropractic
Diets (many)
Distance healing
Energetic healing
Feng shui
Herbalist healing
Iridology
Kinesiology
Magnetic therapy
Manifesting
Massage therapy (from LMT, human touch, healing touch, to tantric touch)
Meditation (awareness/oneness/prayer)
Numerology
Organic living
Past life regressions
Pet therapy
Polarity therapy
Psychic reading
Readings (sharing and studying)
Rebirthing sessions
Reflexology
Reiki treatments
Shamanic healing (soul retrieval session)
Spiritual retreats (denominational, ecumenical, and nonaffiliated communing)
Tantra (study of the ancient practice of spiritual sexuality and "universal oneness")
Yoga (various forms)

APPENDIX C

(Various **Organizations/Foundations/Web Sites** Relating to Healing)
****

Akashic Wisdom	http://www.planetlightworker.com/articles/donnafox/
Conversations with God	http://www.cwg.org
Creative Problem Solving Institute	http://www.cpsiconference.com/home
Embracing Change	http://www.embracingchange.org
Feminine Empowerment	http://mayayonika.org
Healing with the Masters	http://www.healingwiththemasters.com
Humanity's Team	http://humanitysteam.org/
Institute of Noetic Sciences	http://www.noetic.org/
Lily Dale Assembly	http://www.lilydaleassembly.com/
Marianne Williamson	http://marianne.com/
Messenger Network	http://www.themessengernetwork.com
Nanci Danison	http://www.backwardsbooks.com
OM	http://www.dailyom.com
Omega Institute	http://www.eomega.org
Osho Radio	http://www.osho.com/iosho/radio/
Spiritual Cinema	http://www.spiritualcinemacircle.com
The Shift	http://theshiftnetwork.com/
Unity	http://unity.org

APPENDIX D

(MUSIC)

The following musicians are mentioned due to the positive and powerful influence their works have had upon healing in my life. While thousands of musicians could be potentially listed, I have limited it to those whose vision, insights, and inspirations have most deeply supported my life and healthy growth over time. Generally, the overall body of their works is worthwhile; however, in some instances, I refer you to a specific creation of theirs that touched me in a profound way. While many of these artists are no doubt well known, those lesser-known names may prove worthy of your exploration.

Beethoven, Ludwig Von - Sixth Symphony "Pastorale"
Chapin-Carpenter, Mary
DiFranco, Ani
Donovan (Leitch)
Dylan, Bob
Guthrie, Woody
Harrison, George
Lennon, John
McKennitt, Loreena
Minogue, Áine
Mitchell, Joni
One Red Martian - "Late"
Swales, Penelope
Young, Neil
Vivaldi, Antonio
Von Bingen, Hildegard

APPENDIX E

RELATED QUOTES

Consistent with this books purpose of sharing stories that support our mutual healing, I have appropriately conclude by providing quotes from many leaders over the centuries that relate to this theme. I think the collective genius of all our voices combined begins to offer humanity new perspectives that were previously not so readily available for us to see. Consider adding your own favorites as a beginning to a personal healing journal in your own healing process. Regardless, enjoy your path!

****

"If you want others to be happy, practice compassion. If you want to be happy, practice compassion." (The Dalai Lama)

"Grant that I may not so much seek to be consoled, as to console; to be understood, as to understand." (Francis of Assisi)

"Forgiveness is the key to happiness." (*A Course in Miracles*)

"Every patient carries her or his own doctor inside." (Albert Schweitzer)

"Health is worth more than learning." (Thomas Jefferson)

"God grant that not only the love of liberty but a thorough knowledge of the rights of man may pervade all the nations of the earth, so that a philosopher may set his foot anywhere on its surface and say, 'This is my country.'" (Benjamin Franklin)

"The first duty of love is to listen." (Paul Tillich)

"I, you, he, she, we, in the garden of mystic lovers, these are not true distinctions." (Rumi)

"Strangers are just family you have yet to come to know." (Mitch Albom)

"Let no one ever come to you without leaving better and happier." (Mother Teresa)

"Imagination is more important than knowledge." (Albert Einstein)

"Imagine all the people, it's easy if you try, No need for greed or hunger." (John Lennon)

"We must become the change we want to see in the world." (Mohandas Gandhi)

"Humor is the great thing, the saving thing. The minute it crops up, all our irritations and resentments slip away and a sunny spirit takes their place." (Mark Twain)

"I feel within me a peace above all earthly dignities, a still and quiet conscience." (William Shakespeare)

"I think one's feelings waste themselves in words, they ought all to be distilled into actions and into actions which bring results." (Florence Nightingale)

"Everywhere I go I find a poet has been there before me." (Sigmund Freud)

"To the soul, there is hardly anything more healing than friendship." (Thomas More)

"We must learn to live together as brothers or perish together as fools." (Martin Luther King Jr.)

"We are not human beings having a spiritual experience. We are spiritual beings having a human experience." (Teilhard de Chardin)

"We allow our ignorance to prevail upon us and make us think we can survive alone, alone in patches, alone in groups, alone in races, even alone in genders." (Maya Angelou)

"Sex and spirituality are one and the same—we are all born through sex, and hence it is through sex that we can make contact to connect back to our spirit." (Lao Tzu)

"Sharing makes prosperity more shining and lessens adversity. (Cicero)

"Keeping your body healthy is an expression of gratitude to the whole cosmos—the trees, the clouds, everything." (Thich Nhat Hanh)

About the Author

Richard Francis Moore (Poet, Speaker, Author):

Addressing themes of healing and inspiration, combined with the intention of gratitude and encouragement to caregivers and all those seeking care.

A 1974 graduate (BS education) of Niagara University, Richard's career has seen him serve in various executive leadership capacities for over thirty years. His career has largely focused on garnering resources for many wellness and health initiatives (often gender related) within the YMCA movement, Roswell Park Cancer Institute, and the nursing profession. Most recently, he directed the philanthropic development program for the State University of New York at Buffalo School of Nursing.

He has conducted literally thousands of interviews with nurses, other health practitioners, patients, and surviving family members in over forty states for two decades. The advice and counsel he obtained from these interviews are an important source of his work, as he plays back the many voices of nurses and healing practitioners in so many disciplines and venues. He then blends their knowledge and experience about healing with his own experiences, offering insight and inspiration by returning his energy with encouragement to all healers. In essence he extends appreciation to support the healers of our world, and examines how these observations can practically benefit our own self-healing. The heartfelt impact of these stories is followed by his reflective poetry as they combine to touch our minds and hearts. Richard connects with audiences, by providing new perspectives on healing within through an informal process of individual healing, thereby assisting our wounded world.

In the simple process of observing different perspectives on healing, we can begin to better understand our own past, present, and future potential. Many viewpoints can bring us unexpected gifts as we discover emerging new approaches. One example relates to themes of healthy gender and a foundational healing for men and women. Renewing respect and honor, we can restore more naturally balanced loving relationships with mutual adoration and awe!

While Richard's writings and speaking presentations emit from a professional perspective, they also draw heavily upon many compelling personal circumstances as a patient and client. Some of these events ranged from tragic accidents, sudden family deaths, a mother's widowhood, and illnesses that included heart attacks, brain tumors, and various cancers. His works endeavor to express the depth of transformational healing and love that is inherently contained within the individual healing experiences we can share together. Richard's hallmark is his down-to-earth, interactive style that naturally engages an audience by simple sharing our wisdom and healing knowledge with each other.

His career path has naturally led to his ongoing effort to honor all healers. It is his intention to express a long overdue appreciation and a deeper understanding for the positive contributions these healing beings contribute to us individually and throughout our world.

On September 2008, with his three daughters leaving the nest, Richard decided to risk leaving his successful career in philanthropic development to follow an unknown path and clarify his percolating desire to write. Since that decision, he has ceaselessly devoted his energies to advance his writings while availing himself to personally speak to groups on themes of healing. Several groups have included nursing meetings in Boston, Massachusetts, Buffalo, New York, and a conference of holistic healers in Sedona, Arizona, and a New York State conference of Gold Star Mothers of America.

Mr. Moore lives in Grand Island, New York, with Ann, his loving partner of forty years. He is the father of three grown daughters, and five granddaughters. He continues to grow with this lifelong blessed feminine theme, which also includes his three sisters! Richard's late mother, Norma, the 1920s daughter of an immigrant mother, was widowed with nine children at a young age, and was never able to realize her desire to become a nurse. His observations of how his mom was challenged by age-old cultural conditions so harmful to woman (and men) for so long have clearly impacted and influenced his poetry in themes of gender, forgiveness, healing, and love. Two of Richard's three sisters are career nurses. One of his daughters is a nurse in Michigan.

My wife Ann and I

My Mom and Dad centered, eight siblings; with me being at far right. 1961

(Mom 1920-2000)

Our Three daughters

For additional information on many related aspects of
healing, I encourage you to visit my Web site:
www.healingliterature.com
Here you will find a free blog inviting world participation
to share stories and experiences that might support each
other in the many different areas of healing.